CONCILIUM

Religion in the Seventies

CONCILIUM

Concilium 114 (4/1978): Practical Theology

EVANGELIZATION IN THE WORLD TODAY

Edited by
Norbert Greinacher
and
Alois Müller

A Crossroad Book
The Seabury Press · New York

1979
The Seabury Press
815 Second Avenue
New York, N.Y. 10017

Library of Congress Catalog Card Number 78-66134
ISBN: 0-8164-0393-7
IBSN: 0-8164-2610-4 (pbk.)
Printed in the United States of America

CONTENTS

Editorial

EVANGELIZATION and the missions—any mention of them nowadays raises a multitude of questions and problems which are evidence of a major crisis. It is both theoretical (how the Church understands its missionary work) and practical (what is being done in the 'missions').

The problem of trying to talk about the missions shows how uncertain the whole area is. Perhaps a good starting-point is the definition offered in the 'Cordeiro Report' of the Bishops' Synod held in Rome in 1974: 'Evangelization is the proclamation of the joyous message of salvation to all men through words, deeds and life itself'.[1]

Is that kind of evangelization still meaningful today? Is there any chance of it succeeding? Is it perhaps so laden with the guilt of centuries that it has lost all credibility? Perhaps it is more Christian for Christians to encourage people to practise holiness in the religion they have inherited. We shall examine a few difficult aspects of this problem.

The Christian Churches all over the world are increasingly in the minority. Even when we look at the numbers of those baptized, their share of the swiftly increasing population in all continents of the world is constantly diminishing. The centuries-old interest of the Church in evangelization seems to have proved unsuccessful. The hitherto dominant position of the western Churches in relation to the 'mission Churches' has led to tension and conflict all over the world. In connection with the political emancipation of the non-European nations, the predominance of the European Churches has been ever more fiercely questioned. There is an ever-stronger demand that the indigenous national Churches should become the subjects of their own histories and therefore independent of other Churches.[2]

For the most part, the indigenous non-European Churches have not yet discovered an identity of their own. Such a quest for identity has been made almost impossible to date by the far-reaching association with colonization of the European Churches' efforts at evangelization. But to discover an independent identity in church structures, spirituality, theology, liturgy and so on, much time and even crises are necessary.

Paul Tillich indicates another touchy point. 'It should be a principle of evangelization to show people on the periphery or outside the Church that the symbols through which the Church presents itself answer the question in the existence of every human being . . . They [the people of our own time] have to feel that Christian symbols are in no way absurd or unacceptable for thinking and questioning people in our times, but that they point to what really and absolutely concerns us: to the ground and meaning of our existence and of existence altogether'.[3] It would appear, however, that evangelization is succeeding in doing this less and less. Either answers are given to questions which are of no concern to anyone, or the answers of evangelization to our contemporaries' fundamental questions are irrelevant or incomprehensible.

In theory and in practice the question of the association between evangelization and the social and political liberation of the oppressed is increasingly urgent. If it is true, as one section of the World Missionary Conference in Bangkok (29.12.1972 to 8.1.1973) declared, that the salvific work of the Church has four social dimensions (first, the struggle for social justice and against exploitation; second, the struggle for human dignity and against political repression; third, the fight for solidarity as against alienation; and fourth, the fight of hope against despair in every person's life),[4] then the consequences for the evangelization of the Churches are very important.

The 1974 Roman Synod showed clearly that the evangelization of the Catholic Church was in a crisis. The reports of the discussions and the final documents reveal the uncertainty and impotence of the synodal bishops before the immense problems with which evangelization is confronted in the modern world. This *Concilium* should show in some detail how unconvincing the apostolic exhortatio *Evangelii nuntiandi* of Pope Paul VI (1975) has proved to be.

The World Missionary Conference of the World Council of Churches in Bangkok (1972–3) was thought by some people to be a turning-point in the Christian world missions. The relevant problems were certainly examined in a very courageous fashion at that conference. But even there people were very far from a commonly agreed conception of the problem.[5] Therefore some participants asked the missionary Churches to declare a moratorium. They were asked to cease sending people and money at least for a time, in order to help the mission churches to reach a condition of near autonomy.

A moratorium on evangelization? Anyone who is convinced that the person and interests of Jesus and their historical tradition give a convincing answer to the question of what really concerns us, cannot agree to such a moratorium. That does not mean that this request of the Bangkok Conference should not be examined quite responsibly in its context; on the contrary. But a Christian Church loses its right to exist if it is no longer missionary. Of course we all have to rethink our evangelical strategies and look for new ways after painful experiences. Evangelization in the world today has a lot in common with the efforts of one lover to attract another. Nothing can be done by force or threats, by taking advantage of another person's dependent situation, by guile and craft. But loving behaviour that demonstrates the rightness of the declarations made, is convincing and gives rise to a new credibility.

NORBERT   GREINACHER
ALOIS MÜLLER

Notes

1. *Herder-Korrespondenz,* 28 (1974), p. 649.
2. J. Moltmann, *Neuer Lebensstil. Schritte zur Gemeinde* (Munich, 1977), p. 134.
3. 'Die religiöse Substanz der Kultur', in *Gesammelte Werke* IX (Stuttgart, second edition, 1975), p. 108.
4. *Herder-Korrespondenz,* 27 (1973), p. 209.
5. Cf. *Herder-Korrespondenz,* 27 (1973), pp. 206–9.

Pheme Perkins

The Missionary Character of the Church in the New Testament

THE CONTEXT

A REMINDER of the shape of early Christianity should preface any treatment of New Testament views on an ecclesiological topic. We tend to associate 'Church' with world-wide, institutional structures, whereas the New Testament Church was a pre-institutional religious movement. Its small communities lacked world-wide organization, uniform patterns of internal authority, socio-political influence, and—at least after the break with Judaism—national or ethnic identity. All members had been brought up in other religious traditions. When we keep this genuine minority status in mind, early Christian claims about Jesus as saviour of the world have an entirely different sound. One is almost tempted to ask how they conceived of such a thing.

Their reflections on mission were prompted by questions different from our own. First, if Jesus was messiah, why did Israel reject him? Though Old Testament references to Israel's rejection of the prophets could serve as *ex post facto* explanations, the dilemma remained. Old Testament messianic imagery promised a time when Israel would turn wholeheartedly to God and salvation would be definitively achieved. Rejection was not part of the messianic project. Israel's exemplary obedience in the last days might then bring the Gentiles to worship her God (Isa 49:16; 55:5). Instead Israel rejected her messiah, but the Gentiles followed him. Their admission to Christian communities led to other questions. On the practical level, was Christianity a Jewish sect? Did Gentile converts thereby become Jewish proselytes? Once that question was decided in the negative, Christianity was bound to go beyond Judaism. If Gentiles could become Christians without becoming Jews, then it had to be possible to articulate the Christian message in non-Jewish terms and symbols. (Hellenistic Judaism had already struck paths that Christians could later follow.) Or, in contemporary terms, mission and cultural imperialism need not be linked. The New Testament would seem to encourage attempts to formulate indigenous expressions of Christianity. People can be Christians without being western Europeans. On the other hand, no biblical author would suppose all religions to be equal, and no New Testament author that religion is irrevocably tied to a specific culture or national character. The Christ is always preached as saviour of the nations.

EXEGETICAL CONSIDERATIONS

Jesus clearly limited his preaching to Israel; calling her to repent in view of the imminent rule of God. However, his preaching did insist that the kingdom was open to all: tax-collectors, sinners and even Gentiles would be included (Mt 8:11; 25:31-46).[1] New Testament traditions associate the Gentile mission with the commissioning of the disciples by the Risen Jesus (Mt 28:16-20; Lk 24:47; Acts 1:8; Jn 20:21; 21:6).[2] R. Fuller suggests that the tradition of an appearance to James (1 Cor 15:7) derives from a tradition initiating a mission to the Jews in Jerusalem. A similar tradition may lie behind Matthew 10, but the evangelist has omitted the end of the story, since by his time the mission to the Jews was a failure (cf. Mt 5:10ff; 22:6; 23:34-39; Rom 10:21).[3] Galatians 2:7f and Acts 8:4ff suggest that both missions co-existed. Stendahl argues that even by the time Paul wrote Romans, he could see that Christianity was becoming a Gentile movement. His teaching on justification was to explain how they could become heirs of God's promises to Israel, while chapters 9-11 wrestle with the problem of the co-existence of the two communities in the plan of God. He insists that this peculiar situation of Gentile acceptance and Jewish rejection is part of God's eschatological plan.[4] But, contrary to the view occasionally attributed to him, Paul will never say that God has rejected Israel. Somehow God will bring into being a people of both Jews and Gentiles. Hence Gentile Christians are warned not to feel superior to the Jews who have for the time being rejected the messiah. God's plan still includes the salvation of Israel. He has reversed the expected order of conversion in order to include the Gentiles as full heirs to the promises of Israel. They will not be condemned as sinners, nor will they be second-class spectators of Israel's glory as most Jews thought. A pre-Pauline formula in Romans 3:25f ties the salvation of the Gentiles with

God's accepting the death of Jesus as a sin-offering for them. Paul includes Jews as recipients of that sin-offering: all are made righteous by it and not by the Law.

Paul's own mission to preach this salvation among the Gentiles is derived from a commission of the Risen Lord (Gal 1:12-16; 1 Cor 15:8; Rom 15:15-19). Romans 15:7-13 sets the inclusion of the Gentiles within the ethical context of hospitality. They should perceive their status in Israel as that of guests. By showing God's fidelity to the promises made to Israel, Christ has made it possible for the Gentiles to share those promises. The practical side of that indebtedness will be the contribution made by Paul's Gentile converts to the poor at Jerusalem (15:27). But Paul can also speak of himself as indebted to the Gentiles (Rom 1:11-16). P. Minear has pointed out that he conceives of a triadic relationship of indebtedness. All are indebted to Christ for salvation. The Gentiles are indebted to Israel whose promise they can now inherit. Israel to the Gentiles for her eventual conversion (11:13f). Paul is indebted to them for the ministry he has received. Therefore, all are called to give thanks to God for his salvation.[5]

Matthew 28:16-20 is a key passage for our discussion.[6] Most scholars agree that it contains three traditional sayings: Jesus' authority as exalted Lord (18b); the apostolic commission (19-20a), and the promise of Jesus' presence (20b). The command to evangelize is a Matthean reformulation of an earlier tradition. For example, 'make disciples' is his language and probably replaces a traditional expression like 'preach the gospel.' But they disagree as to how Matthew understands the passage. Bornkamm claims that aside from seeing the command as fulfilling Matthew 24:14, the evangelist is not interested in its missionary implications. He is interested in instructing the Christian community throughout. For him, the significance of this passage lay in the eternal validity given the word of Jesus; not in the command to make disciples. All who join the Christian movement must adhere to the word of the earthly Jesus.

Others argue that Matthew does have the Gentile mission in view.[7] They are divided over whether or not he intended to include Israel among 'the nations.' Some argue that the replacement of Israel by the Church in Matthew indicates that the time of salvation for Israel has ended. They point out that the word $ethn\bar{e}$, 'nations', usually refers only to non-Jews. Matthew knows that the post-resurrection mission to the Jews failed (8:10-12; 22:6; 23:34-39); thinks that the only future left for Israel is God's judgment; and is using this passage to show that the disciples have been commanded to leave Israel (contrast 10:5) and go to the Gentiles.[8] J. Meier contests that reading by arguing that $ethn\bar{e}$ means non-Christians in 20:25f and 24:9 and the whole world in 24:14, and refers to the Church in 21:43. Therefore, he argues that the mandate to evangelize includes Israel—now reduced to the status of a nation like the others. But even if one grants the divergent meanings of *ethnē* in Matthew, the tradition behind this pericope referred to the Gentile mission, and there is no indication that Matthew understands it differently. The expression *all nations* occurs in the commission at Luke 24:47. S.G. Wilson suggests that it came into the tradition from an apocalyptic understanding of the preaching to the Gentiles as a sign of the new age as in Mark 13:10.[9]

Luke, as is well-known, turns the mission to the Gentiles into the age of the Church and portrays it as an orderly progression outward from Jerusalem. He recasts the commission to fit that understanding and now includes the Gentile mission along with the sufferings of the messiah as one of the things prophesied in Scripture (24:45f; cf. Lk 2:30-32; 3:6; 4:21, 25-27; Acts 15:14). The coming of the Spirit heralds the time of the Church and the Gentile mission; not the end (Acts 1:1-8; 8:29; 10:11f; 16:6). Luke clearly could not imagine a Church without missionary activity.[10] In his scheme, preaching to the Gentiles followed Israel's rejection of the message (e.g. Acts 13:46-48; 18:8; 22:17-21; 28:28). Arguments from prophecy (cf. 15:14-17) are used to imply that that mission fulfils God's promises to Israel.[11] Unlike Paul, Luke is not troubled by Israel's continued existence as a 'chosen people'.[12]

The sermons addressed to Gentiles mix Hellenistic Jewish and Greek philosophical language (Acts 14:15-17; 17:22-34).[13] Here the religious experience of paganism is positively assessed as a preparation for the gospel. The Areopagus speech suggests that a Gentile can pass directly from his or her religious tradition into Christianity without adopting the salvation history of Israel—the latter, a favourite theme in speeches to Jews. God's universality guarantees the universality of the Christian message of salvation.[14]

The Gospel of John presents a very negative picture of the relations between Christians and Jews. The latter are consistently cast not only as opponents of Jesus but as enemies of Moses, Abraham and even God, himself. This hostility may have resulted from severe Jewish persecution of Christians (cf. Jn 16:1-4a). Therefore, it is difficult to tell whether or not John envisages a continuing mission to the Jews. The gospel does exploit Hellenistic tendencies toward religious universalism in portraying Jesus as the fulfilment of all human religious aspirations.[15] Pre-Johannine traditions in its resurrection stories preserve the familiar connection between a commissioning by the Risen Lord and apostolic mission (Jn 20:19-23; 21:1-13).[16] But the evangelist himself presents a pre-resurrection commissioning of the disciples in the farewell discourses (cf. Lk 22:35ff). Jesus had predicted the Gentile mission and associated it with his crucifixion-exaltation, the return to the Father (Jn 7:34f; 10:16; 12:20f, 32). He now commissions the disciples to act as his envoys in the world just as he had been sent by the Father (e.g., 13:16-20; 15:20-25; 17:11-20; the post-resurrection commission in 20:21 has been reformulated in the same language). Those who will be converted by the disciples will have the same faith; the same relationship with the Father, and the same mission (17:20-23; 20:29).[17]

The inner community concerns of 1 John have led some interpreters to picture the Johannine Church as alienated and closed off from the world; a narrow sectarian group.[18] The commissioning language of the discourses suggests otherwise. Although the disciples are to expect hostility and rejection, their mission to the world defines what the Christian community is about: it continues Jesus' testimony. Unlike Acts, John does not distinguish the apostolate of 'eye-witnesses' from that of later Christians. True faith in the Risen Jesus is not founded on seeing him (Jn 20:8,17) but on realizing that he is exalted in glory with the Father (17:24). John deliberately leaves the preface to the traditional commissioning story (20:19-23) vague: it applies to all disciples at all times; not just 'the twelve'.

These considerations of the Johannine tradition should caution us against assuming that when the Church turned to deal with internal problems as in the pastoral and catholic epistles, it set aside its missionary stance. J. Elliott's study of 1 Peter 2:4-10 points out the importance of mission to that author.[19] Old Testament quotations in vv 9-10 equate the election of Israel with the salvation now given the Gentiles. Isaiah 43:20f defines the task of the 'elect people' as proclaiming the great acts, *aretai*, of God. This context defines the significance of 1 Peter's use of Exodus 19:6 (vv 5b-d; 9b). Exodus 19:6 is always interpreted as referring to God's people as his holy, elect and private possession. It is never associated with a sacerdotal system in writings from this period. The spiritual (= spirit-filled) house (v 5) and the royal priesthood (v 9) indicate that the Church is the spirit-filled people of the new age. Election now belongs to the Gentiles. The spirit-filled sacrifices to be offered by that people are specified by the guidelines for Christian life spelled out in 2:11ff. They are predominately concerned with how one behaves toward the outsider and not with the notion that 'outsiders' included family members (cf. 3:1). Such behaviour aims to bring 'the Gentiles' (now a term for non-Christians) to glorify God. Hence Elliott concludes that the entire ethic of 1 Peter is based on the principle that obedience to the will of God is a positive witness to the world. The responsibility to present such a witness that others will come to glorify God constitutes the essence of the elect and holy people of God.

CONCLUSIONS

All strata of the New Testament associate mission and Church closely. Further, the question of mission is not only an ecclesiological one. It is Christological and soteriological as well. Salvation is no longer only or primarily for Jews but for all peoples. The risen Christ is not simply Lord for his followers but is Lord of the entire cosmos. That lordship is realized as all people are called to glorify God.

Other features of mission in the New Testament run counter to excessively imperialistic and institutionalized views of mission. First, since the eschatological community must be a community for all peoples, a pluralism of religious expression is unavoidable. Second, the obligation to mission is founded on the eschatological character of the Church. It is a permanent obligation laid on those who acknowledge the lordship of Christ; not simply a matter of human decision or expediency. Third, as Paul put it, Christians are indebted to others, to non-Christians, and, ultimately, to God, himself, for their calling. They should not suppose that those evangelized owe some debt to them or even to the Church: all are joined in glorifying the same God for salvation.

Finally, the complex question of Israel's status as a chosen people was not clearly resolved in the New Testament. Those who believe in Jesus as messiah do inherit the promises of the Old Testament. But Romans 9-11 is the only sustained theological reflection on the problem of the continuing existence of Judaism. Paul concludes on the basis of the Old Testament that God must eventually bring into being for himself a people which includes both Jew and Gentile. He cannot say how, but he hardly means to conclude that God has definitively rejected his people Israel, or that their rejection of Jesus should lead Christians to stop preaching the message among the Jews.

We may conclude, then, that the missionary character of the Church in the New Testament is fundamental to its self-understanding as the eschatological people of God and to its perception that the Risen Jesus is not just messiah of the Jews but saviour of the world.

Notes

1. See S.G. Wilson, *The Gentiles and the Gentile Mission in Luke-Acts* (Cambridge, 1973), pp. 4-28, against F. Hahn, *Das Verständnis der Mission im Neuen Testament* (WMANT 13) (Neuenkirche, 1964).

2. See R. Fuller, *The Formation of the Resurrection Narratives* (New York, 1971).

3. Fuller, op. cit., p. 38. On Mt 10 see D. Hare & D. Harrington, 'Make Disciples of all the Gentiles' (Mt 28:19), in *CathBiQuar* 37 (1975), pp. 366f.

4. K. Stendahl, *Paul among the Jews and Gentiles* (Philadelphia, 1976), pp. 2-5.

5. P. Minear, *The Obedience of Faith* (London, 1971), pp. 102-9.

6. Some of the key articles on this passage include: Hare & Harrington, op. cit., pp. 359-69; G. Bornkamm, 'Der Auferstandene und der Irdische. Mt 28:16-20', in *Zeit und Geschichte* (dksg. R. Bultmann) (Tübingen, 1964), pp. 171-91; B.J. Hubbard, *The Matthean Redaction of a Primitive Apostolic Commissioning* (Missoula, 1976); J.D. Kingsbury, 'The Composition and Christology of Mt 28:16-20' in *JourBiLit* 93 (1974), pp. 573-84; W. Thompson, 'An Historical Perspective in the Gospel of Matthew' in *JourBiLit* 93 (1974), pp. 243-62; J. Meier, 'Nations or Gentiles in Mt 28:19?' in *CathBiQuar* 39 (1977), pp. 94-102.

7. Cf. R. Hümmel, *Die Auseinandersetzung zwischen Kirche und Judentum im Matthäusevangelium* (Munich, 1963), pp. 141f.

8. See Thompson, 'An Historical Perspective', pp. 251-9; Hare & Harrington, op. cit., p. 367; D. Hare, *The Theme of Jewish Persecution of Christians in the Gospel According to Matthew* (Cambridge, 1967), pp. 148-62.

9. Wilson, op. cit., p. 47.

10. Ibid., pp. 47-55; 90-96.

11. E.g. Wilson, op. cit., pp. 166-77; 224f.

12. This lack of concern misleads J. Jervell, *Luke and the People of God* (Minneapolis, 1972), pp. 41-74, into arguing that Luke thinks that the Gentile mission was a success and that the Old Testament messianic order of the conversion of Israel and then that of the Gentiles was maintained. This position cannot stand in the face of Luke's programatic summaries. See Wilson, op. cit., pp. 227-32.

13. Cf. E. Haenchen, *Die Apostolsgeschichte* (Göttingen, 1965).

14. Wilson, op. cit., pp. 215-18.

15. Cf. G.W. MacRae, 'The Fourth Gospel and Religionsgeschichte' in *CathBiQuar* 32 (1970), pp. 13-24.

16. Cf. Fuller, op. cit., pp. 139-74.

17. Cf. My discussion of these passages in *The Gospel of John: A Theological Commentary* (Chicago, 1978).

18. Cf. W. Meeks, 'The Man from Heaven in Johannine Sectarianism', in *JourBiLit* 91 (1972), pp. 44-72.

19. J.H. Elliott, *The Elect and the Holy* (NovTSup xii) (Leiden, 1966).

Heinzgünter Frohnes

Mission in the Light of Critical Historical Analysis

LIKE every other movement of religious-ideological expansion, the Christian missions carry the burden of history.[1] This largely determines its present activity throughout the world. But an unbiassed and serious assessment of history only succeeds when we do not lose ourselves in it, and when we remember that, above it all and according to theology, the mandate to preach the missionary message is not dependent on results or historical norms, support or accusations. The only support and measure is the word of Him who guides the believer through the ages: *Verbum Dei manet in aeternum.*

Whatever we think, the past of the missionary movement is with us, and anyone who would put it on one side would deprive the movement today of both definition and depth. But historians and theologians have to accept that the past must be retained for the sake of the present and yet must remain the past. This is the only way which allows us to understand what was possible at a given time, and to understand and judge the language and deeds of people in the context of their own world.

The question is: How does a historian of the missions manage to embrace points of view, debatable issues and methods under the present heading and within the space allotted to him? When one looks for relevant explanatory models and aids to the understanding of historical developments and present circumstances, one can use the systematic, problem-oriented analysis of events in missionary history which in the minds of researchers and in general opinion are controversial, and which lead to an examination of the structures when such questions arise as 'who is to blame for this?'

I have singled out three events which, each in its own way, show
how the process of Christianization is linked with the general, political
and secular history of the world. These are: 1. the Christianization of
the Saxon tribes by Charlemagne with, as a result, a shift in importance
from the Romanic to the Germanic element in the Frankish kingdom,
which led to the rise of Germany; 2. the mission at the beginning of
European expansion throughout the world in the sixteenth century
when, with the Spanish conquest of the new world, the medieval call to
the crusades was for the first time replaced by the missionary mandate;
and 3. the recent history of mission and Church in Black Africa which
is very closely linked with the history of the African colonies and
states.

THE CHRISTIANIZATION OF THE SAXON TRIBES

At the end of 771, shortly after King Charles became the sole ruler of
the Franks, he tried to put an end to the constant strife on the Saxon
border by subjugating the Saxons. But an incorporation into the realm
was unthinkable in the earlier Middle Ages without Christianization
because the amalgamation of Church, State and society, and the inter-
mingling of the religious and political sphere to the point of ambiguity
in ideas and legal action, were in that age the usual ways in which life
found expression. Baptism was on the one hand imposed by law
whereas, on the other, the King was responsible for the Church's
teaching and order in the Germanic kingdoms. The end of the enforced
mission which as a result of Charles's policy of conquest first stirred
the Saxons into resistance and postponed the pacification of the country for decades, and the compulsory resettlement of whole groups of
Saxons well within his own kingdom, are not my concern here. I wish
to concentrate on the structural understanding of this politicized religious situation, or politics based on religion in relation to mission.[2] We
all know about the violence which was part of what are often called in
literature the 'missionary campaigns'[3] and the way the Church was set
up in Saxony. The generally harsh *Capitulatio de partibus Saxoniae* of
Charlemagne, linking up with old-Saxon pagan law, threatened with
the death penalty even minor infringements of the new politico-
ecclesiastical order. Yet, this violence was in no way typical of the
early medieval mission. All the same, one finds here some basic features which hold for other periods of the history of the Church and the
mission.

One cannot see that Charlemagne understood the spreading of the
faith as the king's Christian duty; Christianization followed, and not
only in the chronological sense, subjugation through force of arms.

Above all, the compulsory nature of the too hurried and mostly improvised mass-baptisms made the task of establishing the faith and bringing it within the ecclesiastical framework more difficult, particularly because of constant relapses. In any case, alternative 'compulsory collective baptism' or 'voluntary individual conversion' was alien to the early Middle Ages; this period was rather marked instead by the custom of Christianization following baptism in the framework of an ecclesiastically-ordered organization of that baptism. Yet, behind this is an understanding of baptism essentially different from that of the New Testament and the early Church.

Formerly, through baptism, a prospective convert joined a particular community of which the bishop was the baptismal minister and the local church the place; baptism had an essentially social implication because of the incorporation into the community. But the early Middle Ages saw the understanding and practice of baptism in a different light: a *vir Dei* endowed with a particular calling no longer baptized for and in the community but in the royal palace. The social, community- and church-orientated features became secondary to the desire of the ruling family to ensure its power. To this corresponded the politicization of the godparents' rôle in the ruling families. When Widukind's struggle against Charlemagne ended with the baptism of the Saxons, Charlemagne made himself the godfather of his longstanding opponent, just as, forty-one years later, Louis the Pious became the godfather of Harold of Denmark. The *familiaritas,* or close bond with the Emperor, was strengthened by baptism and the rôle of the godparents, because only full religious communion could ensure full implementation of the political union. Spiritual sonship and political adoption complemented one another. Until the eleventh century the godparents' relationships between Christian princes and princes who accepted conversion were used as a bond in political treaties by the Franks, in England at the conversion of Anglo-Saxon kings, in the mission to the Slavs, by the Normans and in Byzantium, and were applied to bring princes and populations then outside the borders into a relationship of sovereignty. Thus a twofold *fides,* one related to God and the other to the king, found expression at the baptism of pagan princes; in the act of baptism it was the *fides Dei,* in the godparents' relationship the *fides regis,* with, as a result, a spiritual and at the same time political membership within the *imperium.* This theological concept of the ruler fitted the 'imperial theology' of Eusebius which tried to link the appearance of Christ in a God-willed context with the *imperium Romanum* which, because it embraced so many peoples, paved the way for the Gospel to reach the *gentes,* or pagans. In the early Middle Ages the overlordship of a Christian emperor seemed necessary to remove obstacles to this expansion. In consequence, as later on in the age of discovery, the expansion of the realm meant the expansion of the *orbis Christianus;* from this angle, political activity became Christian missionary activity. Hence the Middle Ages came to see the Christian ruler as charged with a missionary mandate.[4]

The Christianization and religious membership of a whole people were decided and collectively brought about by the baptism of its ruler, proceeding from on high to down below as has happened in the most varied circumstances and in all ages throughout the history of the missions. All this shows that the sacral factor of Germanic political sovereignty has been of the utmost significance for the missions, 'which thereby uncritically allowed conditions to be laid down for their successful pursuit'.[5] As happened later in the age of discovery and in the nineteenth century, political and missionary expansion were inextricably interwoven: Alcuin celebrated the victory over the Avars in 796 because Charlemagne had thereby extended both the *regnum Christianitatis* and the acceptance of God. Although Charlemagne's compulsory mission among the Saxons met with criticism from individual clergy and some groups, there was no rejection on principle, not even by Alcuin, although in his letters he insisted that the voluntary character of baptism should be preceded by intensive instruction in the faith. The sequence of subjection to the victorious ruler and then, in the second place and as a consequence of it, baptism as subjection to the stronger God was typical of the Frankish mentality and was not questioned. It looks as if the missionary process was completely embedded in the matter of imperial expansion, but the ultimate and historically decisive result of the enterprise among the Saxons has seldom been shown, particularly by missionary historians. One did not ask what the Saxons said and meant as compared with what they themselves saw as the embodiment of their faith; those to whom the missions and the proclamation of the faith were addressed were not taken very seriously.[6] Conversion was in the hands of the *imperatores,* not the *piscatores,*[7] and the Church's powerful urge towards expansion did indeed drive it into the whole world but neither only, nor even primarily, to spread the message of the Gospel, administer the sacraments and practise works of charity, but principally to ensure power over it.

THE CONQUEST OF THE NEW WORLD AND THE MISSIONARY MANDATE

In the fifteenth century, while the West was in a state of turbulence, stirred up by the desire for reform and even more by unsuccessful reforms, the same western Europe extended its historical *Lebensraum* to a degree which no other civilization had ever attempted. In so far as

Christians of the West were concerned, the extent of Islamic and Mongolian power had proffered both conditions and incentive since the persistent provincialism of the West had failed to exploit the possibility of Christianizing the Mongolian kingdom before the end of the thirteenth century.

The causes of this European expansion were manifold, and pragmatic and economic as well as spiritual and ecclesiastical. In the same way, the discoverers were recruited from all strata of every nation, and showed a mixture of enterprising spirit, search for adventure, scientific interests, the crusader's mentality, missionary zeal and lust for power. However, the decisive element in the discoveries was not so much discovery as such but the occupation of land with all its juridical-political consequences. Here the missionary idea played a real part in world-history. Just as Luther radicalized the crusade and made it a holy war of all Christendom, a war for the spreading of the faith (something it had never been in the Middle Ages, in spite of all the blurring of the borders with a war against heretics), so the colonial expansion of Spain extended the crusading idea, still operative in the early discoveries, to the idea that when military conquest became necessary it should lead to the spread of Christianity to regions where it had never been heard of. The crusading mandate was replaced by a missionary one in the Spanish conquest of the New World in 1513.[8] When the Spaniards, instead of seeking links with China and mobilizing its resources for a crusade, discovered an unknown continent, they could no longer maintain that the discoveries were, as originally intended, basically significant as a crusading action. So in 1501-1502 Spain, faced with this new problem, had to look for some other way of justifying the occupation of the New World. This justification was found in the missionary mandate, something wholly new in the history of discovery.[9] Only recourse to this general mandate allowed for a regional colonization, the occupation of whole areas, countries and continents, and no longer the acquisition of places for support and scattered possessions. Where the faith had to be spread, all those not yet reached by Christianity were to be missionized. The occupation of territory proceeded from a local to a regional level, with, as a result, a definite and coherent colonial possession.

As time went on, the right to discovery grew into a general right to conquest, in which process the legally determining co-operation of the Pope could be dispensed with, as opposed to the justification of a crusade. The change appears in the proclamation about the Indians[10] which was read out whenever the Spaniards acquired new territories in the New World and which was the juridical basis of seizing power. God made a whole continent emerge from the ocean for Spain, and over this continent Spain's power directly represented God's power, the Church's power, and the power of the 'senora y superiora del universo mundo'. As there was total identification of the order of faith with the order of the world, and therefore a radical oneness of spiritual and secular *régimes,* the Christian faith spread by mere expansion of Spanish rule: missionary duty was a maxim of the State.

But, on the one hand, the rule of God's word and his Church had to be pursued in a basically already legally-ordered world which could not be conquered without just reason, while, on the other hand, the faith which it was the State's duty to spread could not be imposed on the natives by force. Nobody questioned the divine mandate, but it did not ordain how it should be worked out. In practice occupation preceded ritual proclamation: the Spaniards called on the Indians to recognize the Church as ruler of the whole world and to accept the right order of faith and world, willed by God, from the Spanish monarch who acted on a direct mandate from God. To refuse that summons meant war, a just war, and the proclamation made it clear that in that case only the Indians 'would be guilty of the bloodshed and the disaster that would inevitably overtake them'. Making God's will known to the Indians therefore established Spain's right to the New World. The call to the faith with the choice of 'submission or war' was a pre-condition for occupation of territory, which again postponed the possibility of starting the mission. The distinction between conquest and mission was maintained in principle in spite of the evidence of compulsory mass-baptism; indeed, the proclamation made faith a personal matter, not one to be imposed by force.

On the whole, this inextricable interconnection of conquest and the spreading of the faith reflects the way in which the early Moslems spread their faith. This is why Las Casas branded this method of conversion as 'godless and Mohammedan'.

Before the period of European colonial history proper, which started overseas in the last third of the sixteenth century as part of the history of the European powers (in other words, in the age of discovery), the missionary obligation and function appeared to provide the basic justification of European expansion and colonization by conquest, and thus passed into the history of colonialism.

COLONIALISM, DE-COLONIZATION AND MISSION IN BLACK AFRICA

Black Africa (that is, Africa south of the Sahara) only became part of general history in the full sense of the term in the nineteenth century. Before this, interest in Africa was limited to the coastlands, where fortresses were built to serve the needs of those trading with India; this meant a strategical containment of the Moslem world. It is true that the Portuguese tried to settle where they could inaugurate missionary activities: on the Gold Coast, at the mouth of the Congo and on the Zambesi. But this attempt collapsed in the fifteenth century. The more promising (but in the sources highly-exaggerated) mission in West and East Africa at the beginning of the sixteenth century was forced back, and anyway already declining, by the end of the century because of the effects of Calvinist expansion on the Catholic reform movement, even overseas. This development worked in favour of commercial interests at the expense of the ideals of the *conquistadores* and missionaries of the New World. Colonization was no longer primarily Christianization, as was the case when Spain colonized overseas, but a drive to encourage productivity and commerce. A positive trade balance-sheet and the political and economic gain extracted from the exchange of goods and transport became the decisive factors. With the independence of the North-American colonies (which revolutionized life in Europe), and with the end of the mercantilist colonial system, the individual, entrepreneurial European created for himself free access to Black Africa with the slogans of free trade and free movement. Decades of de-politicization and de-colonization were opened up and scientifically and culturally developed as independent discoverers, merchants and missionary congregations moved in.

The systematic exploration of Africa started in 1788. After a preparatory phase, this led too precipitately to the decisive opening up of the continent. This was inevitably a pre-condition for the revival of the powerful expansionist politics of the European powers in Africa, and Africa was judged in international law to be 'legally free' territory. During the last two decades of the nineteenth century—the euphoric phase of European policies in Africa—private commercial and religious enterprises looked for political support in their own States. By 1900 the process of dividing Africa according to regional colonization, with an uninhibited inclination to 'round things off' and to secure the economic future on the basis of Black Africa's economic potential in terms of the nationally-conditioned imperialistic powers of Europe, was already over and done with. Africa was completely in the hands of Europe. The borders of the colonies were completely decided upon without any regard to the African tribes and peoples, their native cultural units, which were subordinated to the needs and projections of the fatherland. Colonial companies took over the function which until then the missionary congregations had fulfilled, and as, to a large extent, the missionary officials and missionaries themselves had done, secularized the Christian missionary impulse by stressing civilization, humanity and progress. Methods were dictated by a colonially-determined racial and cultural conceit which was more evident among the English and the Germans than the Romance nations. These methods aimed at training the natives to be useful servants of the European national interests.

Various nations showed their individual differences in their methods of colonization. Recent and present events show that these differences were of decisive importance in Africa. Even the missionary labour and method of the national companies. clearly reflected the basis and mentality of this system: the assimilative approach of France and Portugal which wanted to turn the natives into Frenchmen and Portuguese; the associative approach which the English pursued under the slogan of 'indirect rule'; and the patriarchal-social-conservative approach pursued by the Germans with the idea of maintaining the order operative on the spot.

All this left its traces on the attempts at Christianization, imposed through the schools or even by colonial law; the more Christians insisted on their exclusiveness, the more the doctrine of faith and society was emphasized against the assimilative tolerance of the Africans. The result could only be greater complications, social tensions, the destruction of the tribal system, and relaxation of family and tribal bonds.

The missionaries of this era demonstrated in their words and action the 'expansionism of a good conscience'; Christendom laid the foundations for a 'rationalism' that would enable Africans to make use of the material goods produced by Christian civilization. The missionary attitude towards Africa landed itself in a peculiar ideology: 'humanitarianism', with Livingstone as its protoptype. It did not primarily aim at moulding African society in the image of industrialized Europe. What was decisive was the ethical content which outweighed the economic interests. The first concern was not 'civilization' but alleviation of the physical and moral conditions which determined the life of the individual and of society. The 'natural man' of the Enlightenment period, the native as a raw primitive human being, yielded to the human being in need.

This attitude is met with today. The way in which the missionary and the European at large identify themselves with 'civilization' is only a psychological aspect of a basic problematic situation: What is the attitude of Europe (including the Churches) to 'the Third World'? From the nineteenth century particularly this attitude was no longer explained by reference to some natural and universal Reason, as still happened in the eighteenth century, but was explained by a theory of history—in Christian-theological terms: salvation history—of which the West appeared to be the peculiar result.[11] The secularized and theologicized ideology of the good conscience which had justified the politics of assimilation and rule was not queried until the first World

War, while the second World War paved the way for a basic political revision which since 1958 has resulted in a series of independence declarations.

This is a very rough outline of the history of European colonialism in Black Africa and of the recent and continuing political, spiritual-cultural and socio-economic decolonization. The implied trend towards decentralization is beginning to affect a hidden and still flourishing imperialistic ethnocentrism[12] by means of a number of scientific disciplines, including the historiography of Church and mission. It is in this context that the ecclesiastical history of the missions and of overseas expansion must be seen.[13] Colonialism and decolonization must be seen as a whole and not just as a series of processes which, supposedly independent of each other, can be satisfactorily researched under headings like 'spread of European culture', 'monetarization of the economy', or 'mission'. A certain rhetorical western anti-colonialism subtly incorporates the function of the exotic in the colonial ideology, and thus conceals a theoretical imperialism which judges and examines the situation in a western sense. But the process of decolonization, both as ideology and as an undeniably factual situation, forces us to make a strict and basic distinction between the exogenous change brought about in African society by colonization and mission, on the one hand, and the endogenous trend inherent in the process of decol-onization, on the other. The inadequacy and ideological implications of classical notions like change and cultural contact have often concealed, in the history of the Church and the missions, as in many other scientific disciplines, the fact that a change imposed from outside has nothing to do with the intended spiritual and cultural independence, and that 'African Christianity' cannot be reduced (as so often happens) to the use of traditional elements in liturgical practice, the Africanization of the clergy, and so on.

There are many recent and lively historical publications on the African missions. Because of the lack of historically-trained theologians the authors are almost exclusively secular historians. What I have said here is confirmed by these writings in so far as they tackle the general themes of African history at large and owe their vitality to their integration into the growing historiography of Black Africa.[14] They also show that it is necessary and essential—now especially—to write a 'history of the Church' as a 'history of the missions', to leave some space between the history of the Church and the history of the world, and not to allow ourselves to be confined to the narrow area of mission and Church.[15]

Translated by Theo Westow

Notes

1. A subject which has been dealt with theologically by Gerhard Rosenkranz, *Die Christliche Mission. Geschichte und Theologie* (Munich, 1977).

2. Cf. Reinhold Schneider, 'Karl der Grosze—politisches Sendungsbewuszsain und Mission', in *Kirchengeschichte als Missionsgeschichte* II, 1, *Die Kirche des früheren Mittelalters* (Munich, 1977), pp. 227-48; Hans-Dietrich Kahl, 'Erscheinungsformen karolingischer Reichsmission', ibid., II, 2 (Munich, 1978), and the 'Bibliographie zur christlichen Mission im früheren Mittelalter', ibid., II,1.

3. Cf. Karl Hauck, 'Die Ausbreitung des Glaubens in Sachsen und die Verteidigung der römischen Kirche als konkurrunender Herrscheraufgaben Karls des Groszen', in *Frühmittelalterl. Studien* 4 (Münster, 1970), pp. 138-72, esp. 143.

4. Cf. Georg Kretschmar, 'Der Kaiser tauft. Otto der Grosze und die Slawenmission: Bleibendes im Wandel der Kirchengeschichte', in *Kirchenhistorische Studien*, ed. B. Moeller & G. Ruhbach (Tübingen, 1973), pp. 101-50, esp. pp. 119f., 134, 140.

5. Knut Schäferdiek, 'Germanenmission', in *Reallexikon für Antike und Christentum*, vol. 10, section 76 (Stuttgart, 1977), cols. 492-548, esp. col. 496.

6. The history of the missions includes the history of lack of understanding or misunderstanding with regard to the peculiarity or self-determination of the 'objects of the mission'. Thus it happens that, for instance, some histories of the missions refer to anti-colonial movements as 'atrocious revolts' or as 'mutiny' (cf. Stephen Neill, *Christian Missions*, Harmondsworth, 1964).

7. Rupert von Deutz, *De Trinitate et operibus eius libri XLII* (PL. 107, col. 1048 f.) describes the apostles without power or culture *(piscatores, non imperatores)* as victorious over the power and autonomy of the world.

8. Vasco Nuñez de Balboa (1475-1517) was the first to use the new argument when in 1513 he took possession in the name of the King of the Pacific of the sea of the New World and the New World itself on the Straits of Panama.

9. The decisive element was that the discoverers created new special legal situations as conquerors of the newly discovered regions. Ethical colonial issues, which moralizing authors today have raised in an incorrect and unfortunate manner, played no part. Cf. Joseph Höffner, *Kolonialismus und Evangelium. Spanische Kolonialethik im Goldenen Zeitalter*, Trier, third ed., 1972; Hans-Jürgen Prien, *Die Geschichte des Christentums in Lateinamerika, 1492-1977* (Göttingen, 1977), the chapter on 'Der kolonialethische Hintergrund der Mission'.

10. Worked out by Palacios Rubios in 1513. Cf. Lewis Hanke, 'The "requerimiento" and its interpreters', in *Revista de Historia de America* 1 (1938).

11. Similar discussions are today taking place on the theme of the 'unity of mankind' which is to be brought about through a unitary (European-moulded) world-civilization in the Ecumenical Council of Faith and Order or on the systematic lines proposed by Wolfhart Pannenberg of Munich. An ideologico-critical examination of all this seems urgently required.

12. Often labelled in (missionary) historical research as 'Europeanism'.

13. As an example of the 'metropolitan-ecclesiastical school of missions' (Robert Strayer, 'Mission History in Africa. New Perspectives on an Encounter', in *African Studies Review* 19, East Lansing, 1976, pp. 1-15) see the historically inadequate art. 'Afrika II: Missions- und Kirchengeschichte' in *Theol. Realenzyklopedie* (Berlin, 1977), pp. 700-16. It stresses the European strategies for the expansion of Christendom and the heroic efforts with which the missionaries tried to work out these strategies. In this way the article reflects early colonial historiography. Martin Kähler's question: 'Is church history more cultural history or missionary history?' (1911, id., *Schriften zu Christologie und Mission*, ed. by Heinzgünter Frohnes, *Theol. Bücherei* 42, Munich, 1971, p. 318) should be reversed: Is the history of the mission more church history or 'cultural' (colonial, and so on) history?

14. A survey and assessment of the situation in Black African historical research from the point of view of missionary and church history is being prepared, and will appear in the *Neue Zeitschrift fur Missionswissenschaft* (Immensee, Switzerland).

15. The scope of the task here only referred to extends beyond the ideas expressed by Hans-Werner Gensichen in his 'Kirchengeschichte im Kontext. Die Historiographie der jungen Kirchen auf neuen Wegen', *Lutherische Rundschau* 26, 1976, pp. 301-13.

Alexandre Ganoczy

The Absolute Claim of Christianity: The Justification of Evangelization or an Obstacle to It?

THE PROBLEM

IN THIS article, I shall discuss the absolute claim made by Christian theologians and the Christian Churches: that is, that, as opposed to other religions, Christianity has received absolute religious truth from God in Jesus Christ. My question here is: Can this claim be regarded as an essential precondition for active evangelization on the part of the Churches? Does this claim to absolute truth really promote God's cause, which the Churches have to represent in the world? Or does it have the opposite effect and act as an obstacle to the furtherance of that cause? Or does it lead to both positive and negative results? Does it, for example, mean that Christians, convinced that they possess the fulness of truth and that their religion is 'absolute', no longer bear total witness to Christ, but rather judge other religions as inferior, less true, less humane and of only relative value in man's search for God? Does it also lead the Christian Churches, with their missions, to play the part of 'critical catalysts'[1] without their being 'catalyzed' by the other world religions?

On the other hand, the present crisis in the Christian missions also tends to make Christians think of Christianity as having a relative rather than an absolute nature. Do they not perhaps believe that their religion is as relative as all religious movements that have, in the course of their historical development, absorbed very varied and often alien

elements? Is Christianity not essentially a relative religion because of
its predominantly western—that is, Jewish, Greek, Roman, Germanic,
Anglo-Saxon—character? Is Christianity, in other words, only a partial
representation of God's universal truth? There may also be a wide-
spread conviction among Christians that the infinite and many-sided
riches of the reality of God cannot be adequately expressed by any one
religion, however great its content of truth may be, with the result that
every religion is inevitably dependent on the others if it is to improve
its way of speaking about God.

What will be the result of this? Will our Christian missionaries not
lose both their consciousness of themselves as evangelists and their
certainty of their mission? Should the missions be brought to an end
and replaced by activities based on an exchange between different
religions? But, if this were to take place, would the new approach of
mutual respect and an exchange of dialogue not perhaps lead to a form
of syncretism? Would it not result in a new aim, that of a confederation
of world religions with equal rights, in which the specifically Christian
faith had only one vote among the many others? In other words, a kind
of religious UNO, in which the great and the small powers in religion
had equal voting rights?

These questions can only be answered if the two basic concepts on
which they are based are examined more closely. I shall therefore look
more closely at the theological status of these two concepts—the absolute claim and evangelization—and their interrelationship.

THE ABSOLUTE CLAIM

'Absolute' is, of course, above all a philosophical concept. Something is absolute if it 'is in every respect in itself and through itself and
therefore in no respect dependent'.[2] The truth is absolute for the
thinker, good is absolute for the man who acts, and being is absolute
for the man who exists. In philosophy, certain qualities are recognized
as belonging to the absolute: universality, which sustains the individual, independence, on which everything else is dependent, neces-
sity, which asserts itself against chance, and an unconditioned nature
that conditions everything else. It is obvious that philosophy has always had good reasons for attributing these and other absolute qualities to the one God, although it was not until a relatively late date—
probably in the writings of Nicholas of Cusa[3]—that the noun 'Absolute' was used as a philosophical name for God. The specifically
theological names for God have always, throughout the whole of Christian history, been predominantly biblical. (Examples of such names are
Lord, Creator, Redeemer, and so on.) In these names, it was not so

much a metaphysical position seen, as it were, at the top of the hierarchy and occupied by a being existing in himself and above all other beings that was stressed, as the personal relationship between a God who was active in human history and man.

The idea of the absolute claim of Christianity is also philosophical in origin.[4] It first appeared in the writings of Hegel, according to whom Christianity was the only religion that could rightly be termed 'absolute', because it had raised the essential element of all religion, the union of God and man, to its highest level by professing Jesus Christ as God-man. Hegel believed that the God-man of the Christian tradition certainly corresponded to the historical form of Jesus, but that he also represented a form in which 'absolute Spirit', which was in itself both divine and human, was able to realize itself.[5] As a divine and human reality, the Hegelian absolute Spirit was involved in a dialectical process of self-development. This process resulted in the God-man, who acquired concrete, tangible form in Jesus of Nazareth, thus becoming the foundation of the highest of all religions, the 'revealed' or 'absolute' religion of Christianity. It must be admitted, however, that the word 'absolute' is used here of the Christian religion in a derived sense. Christianity is called absolute only in the sense that it is the bearer of what is (so far) the highest revelation in itself of the absolute Spirit in the form of a historical man. As a dialectical event, however, the death of Jesus revealed new ways of self-development to the absolute Spirit. What is more, religion itself would, Hegel believed, be superseded by philosophy, as an even higher 'realm of absolute Spirit'. For these two reasons, then, even the 'absolute' religion of Christianity was, for Hegel, a factor that could be made dialectically relative. Both the 'further progress' of the Spirit to the 'death of God' on the cross, and the progress of philosophy in the direction of an increasingly perfect liberation from religious 'ideas', make the so-called 'absolute' Christian religion relative.[6]

It would in any case be a very crude misunderstanding of what Hegel meant by 'absolute religion' if we were to regard this as an undialectical absolute, and conceived Christianity as unchangeably supreme among all other religions. Hegel's teaching does not permit us to think of such qualities of the absolute as universality which bears everything individual, independence on which everything is dependent and an unconditioned entity that conditions everything as static qualities. It also does not allow us to attribute these static absolute qualities to Christianity.

The foregoing would seem to indicate that a specifically theological idea of the absolute claim of Christianity can be reconciled with Hegelian dialectics only with great difficulty. In fact, a different direction has been followed by Rahner's well-planned attempt to re-define the relationship between Christians and non-Christians. The point of departure taken by Rahner and his colleagues is an incarnational Christology that is closely linked to a vision of the world. The idea of the universal validity of Christianity is derived from this and at the same time interpreted as an open absolute quality that is ready to be accepted.

Rahner consciously ignores comparisons with other religions and does not attempt to verify them *a posteriori*.[7] He also begins at a pre-philosophical point of departure, with the simple first and fundamental datum of Christian faith, namely that the risen Christ is the absolute and universal bringer of salvation for the world. This basic datum of faith also provides a logical justification for the knowledge that Christianity, as the aspect of mankind that has been eschatologically seized by the reality of Christ, is unique, unrepeatable and definitive and that it cannot be superseded by further dialectical progress.

One striking aspect of Rahner's Christological approach to this question—and one that weakens his position—is that he attaches little importance to the need to justify this knowledge of faith in the message of the historical Jesus. His own basis is in the Johannine teaching about the incarnation of the preexistent Logos. On this basis, he has—like the Fathers of the Church with their background of Platonic ideas—built up a considerable thesis, which has been extended by his followers, of a metaphysical determination of the reality of the world by the divine Logos. Christianity consequently appears as a universal ontological datum of life.[8] It is the depth and the summit of the world of man, the quintessence of true humanity and even human nature itself in so far as it has been redeemed and set free by Christ. Surely there could be no more absolute definition of Christianity than this. Sharing in the fundamentally absolute nature of the universal bringer of salvation, Christianity is identical with mankind that has come to itself. Everything therefore depends on this reality of salvation being grasped, understood and accepted in an act of faith that is in each case subjective and personal. Christian faith can, according to Rahner and his school, possess two actual forms and can be expressed in two ways. On the one hand, there is an implicit, anonymous, hidden expression of faith that is only made concrete in practice and, on the other, there is an explicit, conscious, revealed expression that is made actual and public in practice and in a confession of faith.[9]

What, then, is the relationship between Christianity, understood in this way, and the other religions (which Rahner only considers generally)? Whenever they are experienced seriously and sincerely by men of good will, they are relative seeds of an absolute plant. Rahner himself has commented in this context: 'The seed has no right not to want to become a plant'.[10] The seed, then, has to be brought out of its state as a seed and into its fully-developed state as a plant. This is the essential task of the Christian mission. According to Wilhelm Thüsing, 'Mission is . . . necessary because implicit Christianity must become explicit and in this way come to itself'.[11]

EVANGELIZATION

The task of evangelization, then, clearly has an essential part to play in this transcendental theology of the school of Rahner, as it obviously does not in the dialectical philosophy of religion of Hegel. According to Rahner, evangelization forms an essential part of the Christian claim to absolute religious truth. It is only in the light of that absolute claim that evangelization can really be understood. At this point, however, a certain doubt arises: Is this necessarily the case? Does the Christian religion have to insist on this absolute claim, based on either philosophical or theological arguments, in order to justify the need for mission? Is the situation not very different in the normative sources of Christian faith?

If we consider the proclamation and indeed the whole attitude of Jesus of Nazareth that can be recognized behind the New Testament witness, we cannot say that it contains any appeal to one reality of salvation that is previously given and only has to be made explicit. On the contrary, everything is determined by the radical newness of the kingdom of God that is immanent and voluntarily brought about. If anything can be called 'absolute', it is surely the coming of the kingdom of God, that cannot be produced by any anthropological or historical development, or either forced or prevented by any human power. Only the future reality of the *basileia* has sovereign universal, independent and unconditioned qualities. Jesus himself makes himself relative with regard to the *basileia* of his Father. He wanted to show only the *basileia,* only to be its herald and to anticipate only it. He did not emphasize his own title of Messiah, which might have expressed his unique and absolute quality with regard to the kingdom that was to come. He acted in a messianic way and probably lived consciously as the Messiah, but he certainly did not strive after the name of Messiah. Jesus' evangelizing and kerygmatic way of speaking always points away from himself and towards God alone[12] and his practical aim was the welfare and salvation of the poor, the captives and the sinners (see, for example, Mk 1:14; Lk 4:18; 8:1) of his own environment. To this end he devoted his full power in the task of spreading his eschatological message and his prophecy and promise for the future. His work of evangelization was essentially a theocentricity that was radically anthropocentric in practice and in no sense a sublime egocentricity.

These essential aspects of the work of evangelization remained intact in the period following the Easter event, when Christian attitudes were dominated by the conviction that the resurrection was the fulfilment of the kingdom of God in the risen Christ and in him for all men. According to Paul, for example, the evangelist ought to be nothing but 'the mouth of God revealing himself and proclaiming his salvation'.[13] The evangelist too should not boast messianically, but should perform a messianic service, proclaiming God's absolutely new victory over death, evil and sin.

It hardly needs to be emphasized that the apostles also carried out their mission with the same fundamental attitude, always pointing away from themselves and towards God. They saw themselves above all as messengers who were sent by the exalted Lord. Their imminent expectation of the *parousia* did not, paradoxically, make them wait quietistically. According to the Jewish tradition, other peoples belonging to other religions would share in salvation only if they made the 'pilgrimage to Zion', in other words, if they came to and joined Israel.[14] In the case of the early Christians, the opposite was true—there was an emphatic going out to the pagans. The proclamation of eschatological salvation in the early Church was not only a centripetal, but also a centrifugal process.

This emphasis is clearly expressed in the commandment to be missionaries to the world (Mt 28:18ff), given after the Easter event. This commandment goes back in spirit to the openness of the pre-paschal Jesus towards individual Samaritans, pagans and marginal figures in the gospels, to his own attitude of hostility towards all barriers to the unrestricted and universal proclamation of the Easter event to all non-Israelites. It was carried out by the apostles and early Christians entirely without triumphalism. The centrifugal movement of the mission preserved something of the centripetal patience and readiness to accept that was a fundamental aspect of the parables of the banquet attributed to Jesus himself. Despite many threatening aspects, the fundamental tenor of the early Christian mission was, as E. Jüngel has so strikingly said, that God was 'a Word offered . . . Freedom that sets free cannot be pursued in any other way than in freedom. The compulsion of this freedom can . . . only exist in the explicitation of its own dignity . . . It has the compulsion of a voluntary recruitment and a request'.[15]

Another form of evangelization in the early Church was the so-called 'mission to the assembly'.[16] The missionary proclamation of the kingdom of God, which came to be known in the early Church as the kingdom of Christ, tended towards the liturgical acclamation in the assembly *(ekklesia)* of the brethren. This *ekklesia,* which affirmed its existence in the sphere of worship, showed itself to be both the place of arrival and the place of departure of evangelization. It was 'the place where the evangelized were brought together and prepared', although it did not provide an infallible guarantee of their salvation.[17] There is no trace in the early Church of boasting, making the religion of Christ absolute or believing that the Church was the only mediator of salvation. According to the Acts of the Apostles, the Holy Spirit descended on outsiders without the intervention of sacraments or the Church and was effective in those places where divine freedom wanted the Spirit to be effective. The Christian community was conscious of its relative status because of the effectiveness of the Spirit and was called to obedient dependence on the one Lord.

With this reservation (which was formulated by Augustine as *gratia non alligatur sacramentis*), we may say that evangelization is at the same time a 'sacramentalization'. It generally results in the baptism of those who have accepted the eschatological newness of faith in Christ with faith. By being baptized, they are also invited to share in the Lord's Supper.

If I summarize what I have said so far about the nature of evangelization, it has the following characteristics. There is a consciousness of the radical newness and irreducibility of the saving message of the risen Christ. This leads to a memory of the living example of Jesus and a deep theocentricity that is at the same time concentrated on the welfare, happiness and salvation of one's fellow men and is therefore a concretely soteriologically-orientated theocentricity. There is also a consciousness in the task of evangelization of man's eschatological relationship with the future and consequently of the temporary nature of all forms of mediation carried out by the Church. Finally, the only absolute aim for the evangelizing *ekklesia* is the *basileia* that is to come.

One important consequence of my summary of the essential characteristics of evangelization is that it is necessary to evangelize actively. It is unfortunately very common in missiology to shorten the New Testament perspective by quoting the commandment given by Jesus to be missionaries to the world.[18] This decisionistic view of the situation in fact obscures the really decisive aspect, which is that the people of God of the new covenant are led to evangelize because of the very nature of Christian faith itself. This faith is a faith in the God of Jesus Christ who makes himself public and manifest. Hegel was right in perceiving in Christianity the 'revealed religion' through which the Spirit at the same time expresses and empties itself and also comes to itself. The New Testament, however, goes far beyond Hegel by presenting Christianity with the four characteristics of message, mission, assembly and *ekklesia* of the sacraments. Because Christians are placed in the imitation of Christ as the messenger, the one sent, the one who assembles from God and the one who is truly present, it is therefore 'natural' for them to be active as missionaries.

On the other hand, the view has to be criticized on the basis of the New Testament witness that the Church 'saves' by its missions those who would otherwise fall victims to definitive disaster. The Church is not a redeemer, not an 'only ark of salvation', outside which there are no real 'elements of truth and sanctification'.[19] The Church would therefore be wrongly advised if it were to construct its theory and praxis of the mission on a modernized variant of the Johannine contrast of light and darkness. Only God can save. He alone can know infallibly who is to be redeemed and by whom. It is also reserved to him alone to determine how much darkness and how much light there is to be both outside and inside the Churches. According to the New Testament, it is the task of those Churches to be the sent people of God at the service of the one who sends and the place and organ of the one who saves and to carry out this task in freedom and knowledge.

EVANGELIZATION AND THE ABSOLUTE CLAIM

The relationship between evangelization and the absolute claim of Christianity can be approached in the following way. In the first place, the Church and theologians would be well-advised to consider seriously the problem of language. The fact that there was no talk of an absolute claim in the evangelizing work of the early Christian community is very significant. A verbal claim to absolute truth made by the missionary is open to many interpretations. To what, for example, does this claim apply? What or who is 'absolute'? The Church? Christianity as the religion of 'fulness'? Christian faith as an absolute certainty of the truth of the revelation of Christ? God, apart from whom there can be no mediation of salvation for any religion at all? Finally, we may also ask whether the philosophical term 'absolute' is really suitable as a name for the God of the Old and New Testaments who was so personally involved in man's history.[20]

In the second place, the problem of history should also be considered by asking the following question: What advantages and disadvantages resulted in the past when the claim to absolute truth was made systematically by those responsible for the Christian missions? I cannot unfortunately give a detailed answer containing many subtle distinctions to this question because of lack of space. We can, however, accept the opinion of many critics of the history of the Christian missions—both

Christian and non-Christian—that more harm than good has been caused by the absolute claim.[21] This opinion is not in the first place based on the frequently criticized association between those working in the mission field and the representatives of the colonial powers. On the contrary, it is a view resulting from an examination of the missionary attitude that the Christian possesses full religious truth and has therefore, on the basis of this possession, only to give, admonish and teach or to purify, save and liberate. What is forgotten in this attitude is that Christianity is always fragmentary and provisional at any given stage of history and that its present historical form always looks forward to the future. Its existence is, in other words, always eschatological and this means that the Christian—and the Christian mission—is often placed in a situation of 'not yet' rather than 'already'. It is therefore advisable for Christian missionaries to be extremely cautious in what they say about possessing absolute truth. Only benefit can result from refraining to speak about such a possession in the dialogue with people of other religions and cultures.

As far as the purely philosophical and theological questions are concerned, we have already pointed to the difficulties that are connected with Hegel's teaching and Rahner's thesis. From the methodological point of view, an *a priori* understanding of the relationship between Christianity and other religions is very questionable, since the latter will never be studied at the same depth and in the same detailed way as the former. Whereas the identity of the Christian religion will be taken seriously and its basic structure will be carefully examined, the other, non-Christian religions will almost always be approached generally and without differentiation, rather as peripheral phenomena around a centre (Christianity), which is the only really interesting area of study. This theory of religions, based on an approach from above and not regarding a careful examination from below as necessary, can have a fatal effect on evangelization. The situation is, however, gradually changing and the identity of the non-Christian regions is taken more seriously. Nowadays, in places where the Christian mission has a positive effect, there is almost always a careful appreciation of the partner religion and culture in whose sovereign territory the work of Christian evangelization has taken place. Whenever this happens, there is no need for an *a priori* theory of the dialectical development of religion to an absolute summit in the Hegelian sense or for an anonymous form of Christianity that still has to be made explicit (Rahner).

Can the absolute claim of Christianity ever be meaningful in the task of proclaiming the Gospel to non-Christians and within the framework of non-Christian cultures? It can, I think, be meaningful only if it is regarded as a demand which the missionary makes of himself. This demand is that he should live his own Christianity to the maximum and optimum degree himself, that he should be a total witness to faith. It is in the fulfilment of this demand to bear living witness that this superlative claim (the veral form of what 'absolute' ought to mean) has a real place. Bearing witness to faith can never be sufficiently convincing or convinced. Only the 'absolutely' convinced believer can convince others of the truth of his faith. Only a Christian who confesses without conditions the unconditioned saving value of Jesus Christ as the possibility and the offer of salvation for all men can have the right attitude towards non-Christians, an attitude that involves a readiness to exchange in dialogue, to learn and to teach.

In conclusion, we may say that the service of evangelization is really a service performed for the one absolute God or, to express this biblically, it is a preparation of oneself and the world for the reception of the kingdom of God that is to come. Faith in Christ results in a maximum imitation of Jesus himself, who evangelized, but never preached himself. This faith also leads to a tireless bearing of witness to the fact that the fulfilment of all mortal mankind has become a promise in the resurrection of the crucified Jesus by God. This coming of God and his kingdom is prepared by the work of evangelization. We bear witness to the coming of the God, who is more than the absolute one in that he comes, in the relative and fragmentary experience of our historical situation of being on the way to the kingdom.

Translated by David Smith

Notes

1. See Hans Küng, *On Being a Christian* (London, 1977), pp. 110 ff.
2. J. Möller, 'Absolut', *Lexikon für Theologie und Kirche* I, p. 70.
3. J. Klein, 'Absolut', *Religion in Geschichte und Gegenwart* I, p. 74.
4. Ibid., p. 75.
5. For this and the ideas that follow, see G.F.W. Hegel, *Sämtliche Werke,* ed. A. Glöckner (Stuttgart, 1927-1930), II, pp. 517-620.
6. See A. Ganoczy, *Der schöpferische Mensch und die Schöpfung Gottes* (Mainz, 1976), pp. 41-47.
7. K. Rahner, *Grundkurs des Glaubens* (Freiburg, 1976), pp. 303 ff.
8. See E. Klinger in his collective work: *Christentum innerhalb und ausserhalb der Kirche* (Freiburg, 1976), p. 15.
9. Ibid. This book is entirely devoted to Rahner's theme of 'anonymous Christianity'.
10. See *Schriften zur Theologie* X, p. 543.
11. See W. Thüsing in Klinger, op. cit., p. 104.
12. See R. Schnackenburg, *Die Kirche im Neuen Testament* (Freiburg, 1961), p. 34 f.
13. Ibid., p. 34; the reference is to 1 Thess 2:13.
14. See J. Margull, *Mission* III A; *Religion in Geschichte und Gegenwart* IV, pp. 974 ff.
15. Klinger, op. cit., pp. 130 f.
16. J. Margull, op. cit., p. 976.
17. See Schnackenburg, op. cit., p. 68.
18. See the articles in *Lexikon für Theologie und Kirche* VII, pp. 454, 460 ff, 480, for the theme of 'mission'.
19. See the *Dogmatic Constitution on the Church* (*Lumen Gentium*) of Vatican II, 8. 2; see also 16, where the need for missions is justified in a one-sided way with the salvation of non-Christians from evil and the 'command of the Lord'.
20. J. Klein, op. cit., p. 76: 'Although the hypothesis of the Absolute is inherent in human thought, it has to be admitted that it cannot be identified with the theistic concept of God'.
21. See K. Jaspers, 'Wahrheit und Unheil der Bultmannschen Entmythologisierung', *Kerygma und Mythos* III (Hamburg, 1966), pp. 9-46.

Josef Amstutz

Towards a Legitimation of the Missions

CRITICISM of the missions is becoming more radical. No longer is it just motives or methods that are subject to scrutiny; rather a process has begun whereby the very legitimacy of the project is called into question.[1] This critical reevaluation stems from a number of quarters: from theologians, from politicians, and finally from the Church itself.[2] The Church's own querying of the justifiability of missionary work is one important aspect of this crisis.[3] Inevitably, too, the problem has now been brought to the attention of a wider public.

THE INDICTMENT

For 'the case against' I am citing briefly the proceedings of the *Gemeinsame Synode der Bistümer in der Bundesrepublik Deutschland* which collect together contemporary objections to missionary activity and reservations about its legitimacy. Their deliberations can be likened to an 'internal synod', a 'taking to court' of the Church's past record and present uncertainty, a self-critical and open discussion of the issues and a formulation of problems, often previously only unconsciously perceived.

The Missionary Church's critique of itself:

The missions are the residue of colonialism. Seeking only to extend the Church's sphere of influence, they simply transplanted Western Christianity, oblivious of the intrinsic value of other peoples and cultures. In their disregard for the religious convictions of those of other beliefs, the missions epitomized Western and Christian presumption. Their approach to non-Christian religions was essentially negative, for

30

they were interested only in securing conversions and they overlooked the fact that adherents of other faiths too could encounter God and find salvation. They failed to take sufficiently seriously God's will for a salvation that was universal and not confined to the visible Church. Speedy annexation was their main objective. In every aspect of their work for the cultural and social development of other peoples, their aim, judged in terms of bearing witness to Christian charity, was too narrowly defined. They sought simply to save the souls of individual men and women. There have, as yet, been no demands for structural change.[4]

AN ESSENTIALLY FAIR JUDGMENT

The preceding critique of missionary activity in the colonial period is in essentials a fair one, and it presents a challenge to the missionary Church of today. Certainly, the complexity of the subject calls for highly-differentiated treatment but it must be acknowledged that the overall view of tendencies and determinants is correct. Of course, during the period in question, there were numerous exceptions, but these, far from invalidating the analysis, only prove the rule. Two further points must be added. Firstly, missionary activity has enabled the Church to maintain a 'global presence', although this has always been somewhat tarnished and patchy. Secondly, the colonial past is being replaced by a new era, whose contours, though hard to distinguish, are already defined. I shall now turn to this period of change.

CHANGES IN THE MISSIONARY SITUATION

The Church has been aware since the end of the nineteen-fifties that the missions are working under changing conditions. (During the last five hundred years the Church's position in the world has profoundly altered.) On the one hand, colonialism and European hegemony have enabled Christian missions from the West to bring the Church to the entire Third World. But its presence is undeniably patchy: countries as large as continents or religious communities with numerous adherents have proved virtually inpenetrable to missionary activity; in some places the Church's presence has always been limited; in the eyes of the mass of the people it is no more than a minority. From another angle, too, the western Church has sustained heavy losses: declining membership and the erosion of traditional areas of influence, brought about by the 'enlightenment' and 'secularization' of many sections of society, have diminished its status. It is on the way to becoming a minority Church. As a missionary Church it has reached a critical stage in its historical development. It is here, however, that 'it begins to become the Church of the non-believers, and begins, too, to become a Church in the midst of the non-believing' (Karl Rahner). Missionary activity is traditionally concerned with the individual and once it was considered enough for the missions to define their task in these terms. Now, throughout the world, the Church is faced with a massive 'dissemination of information' in which the name of God, the father of Jesus Christ, passes unrecognized or is considered but an irrelevant memory. The world over, among the tribes of Africa and in the cities of Europe, the Church must proclaim the good news and bear witness to God's kingdom. This is termed its 'global mission' or 'mission to six continents'.

Both in the Third World and in the West, the Church at grass-roots level is becoming increasingly irrelevant. Inappropriate to present-day realities in the Third World, its presence there contrasts sharply with its 'original missionary situation'[5]. The immense efforts of the western Church are clear to see but real success has remained elusive. The Churches which have grown up as a result of missionary work have failed to achieve autonomy: at every level they are dependent on the western Church and are correspondingly alienated from their 'own people'. In principle, autonomy from the universal Church has been conceded but their striving for self-determination (which has scarcely begun) is beset by difficulties. For the western Church has fallen behind the very movements it generated. The ever-increasing flood of information undermines its social authority and promotes the emancipation of the heirs of the Christian tradition from the Church. This amounts to an 'open society' that is alien to the Church. The world over, the Church is faced with the call to be contemporary and to mediate salvation in a truly missionary way.

To maintain a 'global missionary situation' and to 'mediate salvation through missionary activity' are the combined tasks facing the Church in the Third World and in the West. But here there are unequalled resources to hand: historical experience, co-operation in socially important decisions, and the creative powers and material potential of committed and qualified members. Although a Church's true spiritual potential (1 Thess 1:3) cannot be assessed, and although any comparison of that aspect of its potential that we are able to estimate is still arguable, a tentative result of such considerations is that the Church of the Third World must, for the foreseeable future, depend upon the Church of the West. In view, however, of the nature of the Church as a 'community of faith', one Church must carry the burdens of another (Gal 6:2), one must pursue the good of the others (1 Cor 10:24) and because each lives for the other and must serve the other's growth

Rom 13:2), the Churches are obliged to help one another. 'The global missionary situation' is founded in the mutual system of support which exists between the Churches and which stems from their diversity of resources and their reciprocal solidarity.

The western Church cannot, therefore, abdicate from responsibility for its missions and for the growing Churches in the Third World. No Church is answerable purely to itself; each must accept responsibility for the fate of the others and for the success of their work. The Churches have a mutual obligation to confront their difficulties and to work together towards their common goal. By the same token, contact with one another and the assumption of reciprocal responsibility afford the Churches a freedom from themselves. Mutual co-operation enables them to withstand their individual crises and to dedicate themselves to their true missionary task: their responsibility towards men.

THEORETICAL CHANGES

At a theoretical level, too, there have been a number of changes. During the colonial period, missionary activity was motivated by a desire for conversion *(conversio)* of the 'heathen' and the expansion *(implantatio)* of the Church. Despite a difference in emphasis both insisted on 'the impossibility of redemption outside the Christian tradition' *(extra ecclesiam nulla salus)*.[6] The inadequacy of these motives, however, is now generally accepted. The opening-up of more and more 'heathen areas' and contact with peoples of other religions, coupled with the lessons of experience and the revolution which was taking place within theology as a whole, combined to reveal the inadequacy of traditional motivation and to produce a crisis in the missions.

Changes in the ideology of the missions can be summarily examined under four headings but it is not within the scope of this article to comment on the validity of the arguments outlined.

First, it is God's will that all men should find salvation. The possibility of this has been laid down once and for all eternity by Jesus' death and resurrection. His rising from the dead is the most perfect 'salvific event', made manifest in the word. Through his hidden presence in grace, God offers salvation to all men, a salvation instituted, laid down and brought to perfection in Jesus.

Second, the realization of salvation is obscured by time within this world. Time is marked with the stigma of sin. The human heart is torn 'by a desire for evil' and men's actions are inevitably corrupt; these again are the 'occasions of sin'. The grace of salvation flows from the mysterious inwardness of God into men's hearts and effects a change which annuls his fallen condition and the destruction of relationships. The 'change of heart' transforms and recreates them.

Third, God, in the wake of the 'salvific event of Jesus' gathered together a group of people as representatives of all mankind and entrusted to them the good news of his salvation and the means for its mediation. His promise will be continually renewed and through his grace he will mediate salvation to men and to the world. To bring God's word to all men and to the world, God has gathered men into his Church so as to send them out to all peoples.

Fourth, the Church as witness has been entrusted with two tasks. The theocentric aspect of its work aspires towards the recreation of men, towards spiritual regeneration and towards 'the change of heart'. The sociocentric dimension is concerned with the transformation of human relations, with social structures and with justice and peace. The Church is involved with the whole human race. Its involvement constitutes its mission, its way of serving God's will under the conditions of time within this world.

The preceding summary account of some reflections on the theology of the missions calls for a closer definition of terms. The Church as the community of God on earth has been instituted and assembled to perform a particular task. Far from being 'superfluous', the Church has meaning and purpose. Essentially its task is to bear witness to God's salvation, as finally instituted in Jesus, and to mediate it to the poor and dispossessed. Salvation has a theocentric dimension that is most profoundly realized in the kerygmatic sacramental activities of the Church. The sociocentric aspect of salvation emphasizes that social and political issues are equally a part of the Church's concern. By entrusting to the Church the task of mediating salvation to the world, God has made the Church a partner in his saving work through history. This is termed 'mission' (in the singular).

In order to mediate salvation and to realize its purpose (mission) in the world, the Church must itself be present in the world. This implies the building and foundation of Churches everywhere where they do not as yet exist. This undertaking is termed missionary activity or 'missions' (in the plural). Former missions, however, have themselves become local Churches in their own right (young Churches or Churches of the Third World). As part of the community of the universal Church, local Churches must insist that their 'mission' is safeguarded for they, in their turn, contribute greatly in terms of tradition, personnel and finance. Missionary activity really means a supportive-system of mutual aid whereby Churches or groups of Churches help one another to fulfil their mission.

As part of the universal Church, each local Church has a dual function to perform. First, it is responsible—in both theocentric and sociocentric terms—for the mediation of salvation within a particular area and must take steps to develop and safeguard the survival of its work. Second, it must encourage the emergence of other Churches and ensure that their competence is equal to its own. The founding of Churches and the reciprocal exchange of services among them are two essential aspects of missionary activity.

CONCLUSION

If I am pleading on behalf of the missions, I am aware that I began by assuming that their very justifiability was, at least in general terms, open to question. But criticism should be modified in the light of the following considerations. For one thing, the conditions of missionary activity have radically altered. (Certainly there may be areas where they have not, and, should this be the case, then strong condemnation is naturally in order!) But on balance, such cases are probably rare and the crisis in vocations is hastening their demise. Rapid change in conditions and theory are encouraging the formulation of new practical models. New circumstances are forcing the Church radically to reevaluate its position. In addition, the reforms that are introduced are not taking place in a way that is legalistic or arbitrary but rather are actuated by the following considerations.

Firstly, that there must be solidarity between the Churches. Solidarity is the experience of belonging together and of mutual dependence. The Churches of the West and of the Third World can only accomplish their task and be open to the Spirit where they are reciprocally concerned to further their mutual development and freedom. Solidarity is also the responsible acceptance by the one of the concerns of the other. The problems of the Church in the Third World become also the problems of the Church in the West, which must take the situation and convictions of its sister Church as seriously as she takes her own. The Churches exist for one another and the Third-World Church must be equally deeply committed to the Church in the West. Everywhere, in the north and in the south, the Church must work towards the implementation of the dual dimension of its mission. It must both recreate in men the good news of the spirit of God in Jesus, and spread his justice throughout the new creation. It is not enough for the Church to incorporate within itself both the oppressed and those who merely observe oppression, the suffering and those who simply wash their hands of the suffering, and to designate this a community of faith, a new people of God. 'A truly universal Church may not itself mirror the contradictions of society'[7]. The basic rule of missionary practice is not expansionism' but patient expectation of the new creation and the new humanity, a collective experience and articulation of belief. Methodological models can be found in P. Freire's *Pedagogy of the Oppressed*, in C.R. Rogers' *Client-Centred Therapy* and in H.E. Richter's *Social Practice*.

The legitimation of the missions is a question for the future. Like so many aspects of the Church's work, their justifiability depends on their readiness to reform.

Translated by Miranda Chaytor

Notes

1. Detailed bibliographical references can be found in *Bibliografia Missionaris* (Rome, annually). As an introduction, the following are relevant: J. Galzik, 'Wandel der Mission—Gewandeltes Missionsverständnis', in *Priester und Mission* (1975), pp. 635-58 et passim; M. Dhavamony, 'Mission in der nachkolonialen Aera', in *Internat. Kath. Zeitschrift* (1974), p. 203 n. 1; W. Kasper, 'Die Kirche als universales Sakrament des Heils', in A. Bsteh, ed, *Universales Christentum angesichts einer pluralen Welt* (Mödling, 1976), pp. 33-35, 33 n. 1.

2. See also the Bangkok Conference (1973); the Episcopal Synod in Rome (1974); although the perspective is ecumenical, the plenary session of the Pastoral Council of the Dutch Church and the 1972 Synod of the Swiss Church offer useful discussions of the problem.

3. The crisis in the missions has two distinguishable yet associated aspects. On the one hand it is a structural crisis: in the absence of profound reform, the support-system threatens to fall apart; what is needed is an investigation into the statistical relations between the basis and cadres, between the nations that have been contacted and those as yet outside missionary endeavour: cf., J. Amstutz, G. Collet & W. Zurfluh, *Kirche und Dritte Welt im Jahr 2000* (Zürich, 1974), pp. 25-27. One result of this aspect of the crisis is a drop in missionary vocations and the crises of motivations and relevance for which there is ample evidence: cf., Glazik, op. cit. supra. On the one hand there is a querying of the legitimacy of the missions, of missionary activity in the Third World, which can lead to a questioning of missionary activity pure and simple and of the universal salvific task of the Church. I confine my remarks to the doubts thrown on the missions.

4. *Gemeinsame Synode der Bistumer in der Bundesrepublik Deutschland* 1, (Freiburg, 1976), *Missionarischer Dienst an der Welt*, Nos. 02 and 03; see also L. Wiedenmann's commentary, pp. 801f (n. 221); p. 815 (n. 31).

5. Cf., J. Amstutz *et al., Kirche und Dritte Welt,* pp. 17f., 80-82, 192; similarly, 'Plädoyer für eine neue Kirche', *Evang. Missions-Magazin* 117 (1973), pp. 159f.

6. J. Amstutz, *Kirche der Völker* (Freiburg, 1972), p. 23 n. 46.

7. *Gemeinsame Synode der Bistümer in der Bundesrepublik Deutschland 1, Unsere Hoffnung* IV, 3, p. 109.

Walter J. Hollenweger

The Aims of Evangelization

THE CHILDREN of my colleagues at the university are undergoing conversion. They are invited to parties by the Christian Union, an evangelical organization for secondary-schoolchildren and students, and through the personal witness of their peers they are being won over to this particular expression of Christianity. Once they are converted, the new Christians are introduced to the evangelical way of thinking, praying and living by means of literature, bible study, companionship, and entry to evangelical parishes or communities. The new converts quite often include the children of critical theologians. They are often the more rather than the less intelligent among the schoolchildren and students.

CONVERSION OF INDIVIDUALS

Evangelization has a clear goal for these students and children. For them evangelization means conversion of young people to a particular outlook on life, a specific way of life, a specific Christology and soteriology. These are decisive in the lives of the young converts since they offer them a way out of the jungle of modern pluralism. Most of them know very well that the statements of the theological mentors (who usually have no university theological background) are intellectually indefensible. But intellectual respectability doesn't count for them so much as guidance in life, the *communio sanctorum* which they think they will find in the conventicle of the young converted.

The scholarly literature is to be contrasted with this empirical finding. The fifteenth edition of the *Encyclopaedia Britannica* (1943-1973), for example, offers under the heading 'Conversion' information on specialist legal and financial terminology. A short article on 'conversion-reaction' refers us to the main article 'Hysteria'. As far as the public in the West is concerned and therefore for the theological specialist literature, conversion of an individual as the goal of evangelization is practically non-existent. The conversion of pounds sterling into American dollars is more relevant than the conversion of human beings. Where 'conversion' occurs in a literary sense, it is with only a few exceptions[1] either described, categorized and to some extent 'explained' by psychologists and psychiatrists, or treated exegetically, systematically or historically by theologians.[2] In both cases a false impression is awakened: conversions are something in the past. Nowadays they seem of marginal importance. They can be studied in ethnic and religious sub-groups and in pathological cases. In the Catholic literature they are described as 'abandonment of the life of the world by choosing religious obedience, and passing from one confession to another, especially from non-Catholics to the Catholic Church'.[3]

But conversions are not (as one might conclude from the specialist literature) atypical experiences in western culture. Any false conclusions arise from the repression mechanism of what we call 'science'. Accounts of conversions like those of Paul Claudel, Charles W. Colson, T.S. Eliot, A. Frossard, A. Schneider, R.A. Schroeder, or the Jesus People, do not fit our interpretative framework. They are explained, therefore, as exceptions, in complete contrast to the empirical evidence of Jung, for instance, who wrote: 'Among all my middle-aged patients, by which I mean those older than thirty-five, there is none whose basic problem is not that of his religious attitude'.[4]

In moments of total crisis people hope for complete renewal. But it seldom leads to the traditional Churches. In a few cases the Free Churches, the sects and other bodies, whose philosophies are difficult to pin down, receive the converts; in other cases they enter Catholic or Protestant lay and religious orders, seminaries, theologico-political groups and house communities. The last-named are developing mainly in Catholic circles in the USA, but also in Europe, as receptive groups for converts, and in the future there will be severe tension between the established Churches and these communities. Such tension can be avoided only by means of serious dialogue between these 'cross-confessional groups' and representatives of traditional church structures and academic theology.[5]

As far as the new converts are concerned, as a rule it is not important whether the groups they join offer Christian, Buddhist or Marxist ideologies. What counts is an appropriate grasp of personal integration. The converts do not care whether the integration is real or imaginary. A reality that is merely believed in has—for a time—the same effect as one that is actually experienced. 'What takes effect is real', says Jung.

Theological arguments do not affect this. Even though individual conversion counts as an unsatisfactory goal of evangelization (an opinion I hold too) theological arguments are ineffectual against this position. The following steps seem more appropriate.

INDIVIDUAL CONVERSION IN THE NEW TESTAMENT

First, I should say that it is correct to accept individual conversion as *a possible aim*. It has a considerable biblical and ecclesiastical tradition behind it, both as the 'planting of churches' and in the less reflective, more spontaneous form of the evangelization of the individual without associated strategic considerations of Church growth. On the other hand, however, the exegetical and dogmatic basis of this aim is not so great as supposed by those who would make it the sole agency. Nevertheless, there is no point in talking to these evangelizers in a way that would negate the basis of their Christian existence (that is, their conversion). More appropriate would be a common consideration of individual conversion as presented in the New Testament. Then we get a quite different picture from that most people would like to put forward. One of the most important accounts of conversion in the New Testament, that of the Roman officer Cornelius, is placed strategically by Luke at the point of transition of mission from the Jews to Gentile Christianity; it shows that evangelization is also understood as individual conversion, linking the evangelization of the evangelist with that of the person to be evangelized. What is striking in this conversion story is that an apostle who was called to be the rock of the Church, learnt something fundamental about the Gospel in the course of his evangelizing—something that he had not been aware of before. This naturally brought him into conflict with the church elders in Jerusalem.

The story of Cornelius's conversion (which might also be called the conversion of Peter, in a certain sense) is no exception in the New Testament.[6] That has often been and still is the case, from Peter down to Matteo Ricci, Placide Tempels, the worker priests, Helder Camara and Hans Küng. That is not really astonishing, for evangelization is *martyria*. That does not mean primarily the risking of possessions and life, but rather that the evangelist gambles, as it were, with his own understanding of belief in the course of his evangelizing. He, so to speak, submits his understanding of the world and of God and of his faith to the test of dialogue. He has no guarantee that his understanding of faith will emerge unaltered from that dialogue. On the contrary, since he expects an exchange of trust with his partner in dialogue, he has himself to remain open or sensitive to the arguments of the person who is to be evangelized.

How can anyone expect that the person who is listening to him should be ready in principle to change his life and way of thinking if he, the evangelist, is not notionally prepared to submit to the same discipline? This is the dangerous aspect of evangelization: namely, that the evangelist risks his own faith in the course of evangelization. Evangelists who evangelize from a fixed and unalterable position cannot seek support in the New Testament. They are propagandists and not evangelists.

THE HUMANIZATION OF MAN

When we try to find out exactly what happens in this evangelization process, we can, in the Third World at least and occasionally in our own environment, observe some major extensions of the goals of evangelization by means of what *de facto* happens in evangelization. In that form of evangelization in which the evangelist is also evangelized, many Third World Christians discover that conversion and becoming a Christian occur simultaneously with the founding of manufacturing and agricultural co-operatives, and with the establishment of organizational and social forms which are on the way to the humanization of man revealed by the Gospel. Forms of society and organization, pre-Christian healing and forms of celebration, pre-Christian and archetypal psychological insights and consequent therapies can be used in the service of this humanization. That is the experience reported, for example, by the American anthropologist D.E. Curry[7] of a pentecostalist group in the hinterland of Brazil, for which evangelization goes hand-in-hand with local land-reform politics. The report of his authority Antônio José dos Santos, which Curry gives in a taped interview, is a fascinating yet irritating mixture of naïve credibility and political tactics. The goal of evangelization is described traditionally as individual conversion. In fact, however, it is experienced as a mode of survival of a human community in the inhuman conditions of the Brazilian hinterland.

It is reported from the diocese of Helder Câmara in Recife that other, for the most part pentecostal evangelical groups work together with the Catholic grass-roots communities, and discover together with them the humanization of man as a dimension of evangelization. That is possible because they have discovered in the popular spiritual (and secular) songs of Brazil (not in Catholic or Protestant theology) a means of communication among and between themselves and with those they wish to evangelize. Catholics and Protestants are also in the same objective situation. Further examples from Mexico, Africa and the black communities of North America are to be found in my *Pentecost between Black and White*.[8] These vocal Christians release energy for what Erhard Eppler rightly prizes as 'intermediate technology' because their verbal liturgies awaken the certainty that they are accepted and cared for by God. Hence they advance trust in their own ability to discover things—an ability given them by God. They make room for verbal, theological and political debate. In so doing they defreeze the western liturgical formularies and replace imported thought-forms (among which are not only political ideologies but the aim of evangelization as individual conversion) with the political education of the people of God within the framework of a vocal liturgy for which the whole community is responsible.

In order to give the reader a more exact picture of what I mean by the humanization of man and the survival of a human community in inhuman conditions, even though these experiences are related in the terminology of conversion testimony, I shall go back to the story of Antônio José dos Santos. He says: 'I was born in the state of Alagoas in the city of União dos Palmares. The names of my parents were José Filipe dos Santos and Joana María da Conceiçâo. At the age of six months I was taken to the state of Pernambuco where I was reared. At the age of twenty-one I was married. I married abiding by the laws of the Catholic church and only now have married legally. At the age of thirty-six I accepted the Word of Christ's Gospel. It happened in the município of Pôrto do Calvo at the Engenho São João. There already existed an assembleia in that place and that is where the Lord used me. And I went into the desert to pray for a period of ten months, then I started preaching the Gospel to the people'.

Antônio then describes in detail how he received baptism of the Holy Spirit and was called in visions to become an evangelist. He earned his living as an agricultural worker and evangelized and preached publicly when he had earned enough to keep himself and his family. But he led a difficult life and could not stay longer than a few months in any one place:

> Once more I had to move on, so I returned to Sergipe and Campo Nôvo where my wife and children were and preached the Gospel there. The owner of the farm and his entire family were converted and I started a small congregation. After eight days the people from Santa Brigida who had been converted began moving in over the thirty kilometers trail between the two places. These people fled from Santa Brigida by night because of fear of the Captain of Police, José Rufino, and other people in the town. They came in groups of twenty-five at a time and within a few days there were about thirty families at Campo Nôvo, which amounted to about one hundred and fifty persons. We stayed there together for four years and eight months. . . .

Now the owner of Campo Nôvo farm who had been converted had a son who had been absent for some years in the city of São Paulo. One day he came home and found all of those crentes (believers) farming on his father's property and he began immediately to agitate to have his father send us away upon the pretext we would eventually take the land away from his father and the heirs. Really, though, what he wanted was the improvements we had put on the land in those years of hard work: thirteen good houses, five acudas (reservoirs for water) and a large number of tarefas (unit of land measure equal to three-fourths of an acre in Sergipe) of rice, beans, and cotton. His father finally agreed to his demands and I went to the authorities of the município asking them to try and intercede for us for at least some sort of partial payment for all we had to leave behind. On 27 May 1958 sixty crentes followed me leaving behind everything and we all travelled forty-five kilometers to another fazenda named Belo Horizonte. The wife of the farmer at Campo Nôvo turned against him when he treated the crentes in this manner, and came with us. Today she lives with us here on the Fazenda Belo Horizonte and has brought suit against her husband for her share of the property at Campo Nôvo.

The fazeindeiro of Belo Horizonte was named Agostinho Barbaso dos Anjos and he took all of us in, offering us land. He told us he would sell the land to us so we would never be chased again. But we did not have any money with which to pay. He said that it did not matter. I was to stay and work with the people and pay him as we could. After nine months at Belo Horizonte he gave us a written title by means of which I and all the people became registered owners of 2300 tarefas. We had to work three years more in order to pay for it in full but after this we were free to move onto the property and build our homes on it. This is the settlement we have built, and are still building, and we call it Fazenda Nova Vida (New Life Farm). To the thirty families who moved here with me I appointed a piece of ground, all that they were able to work, and gave them a property document for it. Each family received land according to its size and the number of hands it was able to put to work. The church we have built we call the Evangelho da Paz (Good Tidings of Peace). The public authorities of the município of Poco Redondo, in which Belo Horizonte was located at the time we came, refused to have anything to do with us up to and including this very day. On 24 September 1963, our church joined the Assembly of God igreja-mãe of Aracajú.[9]

According to María Isaura Pereira de Queiroz,[10] the most important function of one of these groups (de Queiroz calls them 'messianic movements') is 'the transformation of secular society . . . the second function is the renewal of the local political play of forces, for the traditional leaders (who no longer earn any trust) are replaced by a new leader'. De Queiroz calls him 'Messiah'. In the present connection the term 'evangelist' will suffice. But he is an evangelist on the Old Testament pattern, for his greatest concern is the survival as a human group of those entrusted to him and saved by him, which is principally in our case the solution of the land problem.[11]

Similar stories can be related about other Latin American and African countries. These facts contrast with what most European theologians would read into the words and ideological development of these groups. This observation applies both to the Catholic grass-roots groups and to the Pentecostal, independent and mixed groups. Today we are faced with the task of a social hermeneutics; in other words, in every case we have to see what function the ideas and concepts in question—whether they sound acceptably Marxist, Catholic, Pentecostal or Protestant—have in a specific social context. The words used by these groups have come to differ from the language and ideas of Europe, even though the European and even transatlantic partners may not be aware of that. Both have lived in separation for so long and have thought differently for so long, that even when the actual words are the same, the language is essentially different—an observation which has its counterpart in German usage in the German Democratic Republic compared with that in other German-speaking areas. Similar 'linguistic pollutions' are to be observed in the usage of various social strata in Britain. Consequently the direct hermeneutical key to these ideas is to be found not in the European history of language and ideas (nor in the history of language and ideas adduced by the universities of the relevant countries), but in the function or rôle of these words and ideas in a specific context. The participants at the second Vatican Council discovered that traditional theological and pastoral terms have a wholly new meaning and function in a new context, when they listened to some of the more articulate bishops from Latin America. At the Evangelization Conference at Lausanne in 1975, Protestants had a similar experience. The words 'evangelization' and 'conversion' were still used but for some they now had dangerous political and socio-political undertones.

HERMENEUTICS IN A SOCIAL CONTEXT

If, however, an identical history of ideas, and the same words in inner Brazil mean something different from what they would indicate in a North American middle-class church or at an ecumenical conference,[12] and if identical terms mean different things when they are used to describe the aims of evangelization in diverse social contexts, certain problems result for theology, and especially the theology of mission.

1. Identical aims in evangelization and identical professions of faith can express both the unity and the non-unity of the Church. In any case they are quite inappropriate to the expression of unity in the present intercultural situation, and to a common description of the aims of evangelization. The question is then one of their replacement.

2. If we look to the structure and hierarchy of the Church for the means of unity, a similar problem arises. We have to find organizational and hierarchical structures which are not merely associated with *one* history of ideas or *one* socio-cultural context (which is then wherever possible presented as universal and catholic). Here the principle of conciliarity would have to be applied not only to the various denominations in the sense of the history of theology, but to the socio-cultural contexts in which they appear.

3. How are evangelists, missionaries and priests to be formed when one has no idea of the context in which they are to operate later on, or if one knows that they will have to work in quite different socio-cultural contexts?

My answer to these questions—which no longer remains within the framework of this short article—is oriented to an intercultural theology which tries to find a common hermeneutical medium in the medium of narrative and of critically-interpreted myth, yet not in such a way that reflective conceptions of the nature of narrative and myth are put forward, but so that stories and myths are narrated in order to exert a critical function that is socially and culturally discernible.

Translated by John Griffiths

Notes

1. Cf., for instance, L. Schmid, *Religiöses Leben unserer Jugend. Eine religionspsychologische Untersuchung* (Zürich, 1960); W. Gruehn, *Die Frömmigkeit der Gegenwart. Grundtatsachen der empirischen Psychologie* (Constance, second ed., 1960); H.J. Baden, *Literatur und Bekehrung* (Stuttgart, 1968).

2. Cf., for instance, L. Wyatt Lang, *A Study of Conversion* (London, 1931); W. Sargent, *Battle for the Mind* (London, 1957); W.B. Thomas, *The Psychology of Conversion* (London, 1935); A.C. Underwood, *Conversion* (London, 1925); H.J. Weitbrecht, *Beiträge zur Religionspathologie insbesondere zur*

Pathologie der Bekehrung (Heidelberg, 1968). Extensive bibliography in the article 'Bekehrung' in the *Theologische Realenzyklopädie* (Berlin, fourth ed., in preparation).

3. W. Keilbach, *Bekehrung,* II in LThK, II (1958, second ed.), pp. 137f.

4. R. Hostie, *Analytische Psychologie en Godsdienst* (Utrecht, 1955), pp. 210 ff.

5. *Neue transkonfessionelle Bewegungen: Oekumenische Dokumentation,* III (Frankfurt, 1976); *Religiöse Gruppen* (Düsseldorf, 1976). Discussed in W.J. Hollenweger, 'Die Kirche für andere—ein Mythos?' in *Evangelische Theologie* (1977).

6. See W.J. Hollenweger, *Evangelism Today* (Belfast, 1976).

7. Donald Edward Curry, 'Messianism and Protestantism in Brazil's Sertao', in *Journal of Inter-American Studies and World Affairs,* 13/3 (July, 1970), pp. 416-38.

8. W.J. Hollenweger, *Pentecost between Black and White: Five Case Studies on Pentecost and Politics* (Belfast, 1974).

9. At the express wish of Antônio José dos Santos, all persons and places are given their actual names.

10. María Isaura Pereira de Queiroz, *Movimentos Messiânicos* (Sao Paulo, 1962), quoted in Curry, loc. cit., p. 429.

11. These and other cases studied are treated in more detail in W.J. Hollenweger, 'Conversion: L'Homme devient homme', in *Chemins de la Conversion: 45ième Semaine de Missiologie de Louvain* (Brussels, 1975), pp. 78-101.

12. Jörg Müller, *Uppsala II. Erneuerung in der Mission (Studien zur interkulturellen Geschichte des Christentums,* 10) (Frankfurt, 1977), especially pp. 68, 40.

Yves Raguin

Evangelization and World Religions

THE VERY essence of a religion is to provide a means of salvation, and in this case salvation is understood as liberation from the present, temporary, imperfect and usually unfortunate condition of life.

For a Christian, salvation is liberation from sin and access to eternal life in and through union with Jesus Christ. Christianity insists firmly on the sinful condition of man, but much more on the saving power of Christ the saviour. But in other religions, Buddhism for instance, there is properly speaking no saviour, and man is the proper agent of his own salvation. Instead of speaking of sin, Buddhism speaks of *karma:* that is, of retribution for actions which engage man in the indefinite process of deaths and rebirths, up to the point of access to the state of *nirvana,* which is definitive salvation. This salvation is the permanent and happy state of liberation from the law of *karma.* That is the basis of the theory of salvation in Buddhism.

We believe that we discover our salvation in Christ, because God alone is able to free us from all our sins so that we can enter into eternal life. But we are so used to talking about salvation in Christ that we tend to forget the basic question of salvation outside Christendom. Are Christians the only people who are saved?

The problem raised here may be formulated thus: since all religions offer a way to salvation, what is the theological value of those religions in relation to the 'salvation of man'? Once this problem has been examined others are raised, like that of evangelization, or even of the promotion, on a temporary basis, of another religion.

THE ACTION OF GOD IN HISTORY

If we say that God has come to save mankind, we mean first that our present life is a state of test, where man is in constant danger of losing himself. It means also that God offers his hand to man in order to free

47

him from sin and to allow him to attain to a life that will be happy for all eternity. We find ideas more or less equivalent to this in all religions.

But when we say that there is salvation only in Christ, what salvation are we talking about? Do we mean that if someone does not believe in Christ he will not enjoy eternal life and will disappear for ever? Will this everlasting life of which Christ speaks have some special character through being offered to us because we have believed in him? It would seem that the problem has been pushed into a corner of the Christian consciousness. Yet now that we are really face to face with the major religions and all their riches, we have to ask the question all over again. What do we mean when we speak of salvation in Christ—a salvation that we find nowhere else?

To understand and interpret the divine intentions, we have to look at human history. Two facts seem of prime importance. The first is that mankind has always looked for a way of salvation. That has given rise to all the religions and moral rules we know. The second is that Christ came very late, or relatively late in human history. That would seem to indicate that salvation in Christ is offered quite gratuitously to mankind. The coming of Christ is necessary for the salvation of mankind as a whole, without that meaning that in order to be saved every human being should know Christ and recognize him as saviour.

If that is the meaning of the late arrival of Christ in history, and if God wants all men to be saved, we must conclude that salvation has always been offered to everyone in his particular religion. If human history really gives us a message from God that is certain, all religions have a part to play in God's plan, and a saving power. The problem is to decide the relation of their mission and power to Christ's own mission and power.

In addition, in order to bring us salvation, the Word of God became incarnate in a specific man. Jesus of Nazareth is no ideal worked out by the human spirit. He lived in a small corner of the world, restricting his activity to his own people and more especially to a very small group of disciples and friends. He did not claim to make his message directly universal but left that mission to his apostles. Hence his message was passed on in accordance with the rhythm of history, with all its advances and setbacks.

Since, in addition, Christ's message has to undergo the misfortunes of mankind, it can lose credibility in the eyes of men. In this case it is difficult to require non-Christians to adhere to a doctrine whose majesty they cannot understand. Those who reject Christ for that reason may act in quite good faith, and God offers them a form of salvation through the mediation of their own religion. It seems very difficult to reach any other interpretation of salvation history.

THE THEOLOGICAL VALUE OF THE MAJOR RELIGIONS

The theological value of religions is to be found in their capacity to allow us to acquire knowledge of God and their value in expressing his mystery. The most extreme case is certainly Buddhism which absolutely rejects any idea of God. But we have to try to understand this fundamental position of Buddhism. The Buddha wanted to attack the Brahmanic attitude, which was wholly oriented towards the higher powers. He wanted to guide men towards awareness of their entirely personal responsibility in the law of *karma*. Moreover, though Buddhism rejects the concept of God, it nevertheless recognizes the existence of an Absolute. It is in this direction that we have to look in order to understand the meaning of salvation in this religion. Salvation is seen basically as the experimental realization of personal identity with that Absolute. If the distinction between man and the Absolute disappears in the actual realization of salvation, it is nevertheless something which is fulfilled on the way to the realization of that identity.

All religions have a more or less developed theology. Some of them say more about God in certain respects than others can do. To imagine that all religions have the same capacity to 'reveal' mystery does not seem very objective. If individuals and groups do not all have the same capacity to experience God and express that experience, the same is true of religions.

What I am advancing here is what Christ gave us to understand: namely, that he brought a revelation of the mystery of God which had never been made before then. That is what he constantly impressed on his enemies and on his disciples. He presents himself as in the dual line of the explicit revelation given to Israel and the less explicit revelation given to all mankind. He came so that men should have life in abundance.

If the other religions did not have the benefit of the explicit revelation made by Jesus Christ the incarnate Word, there is nevertheless the revelation made in the core of each man's heart by God's word. The Incarnation made possible a particular form of revelation, but it did not reduce the others to nothing. God works by adding, developing, explaining, but not by wiping out. We may apply to everything of this kind that has been produced before the Incarnation and which is produced now outside the Christian world, the words of Christ: 'I have not come to put down, but to build up'. (Mt 5:17).

What we hear at the beginning of the gospel of John on the action of God's Word in the world before the Incarnation explains to us something of the way in which the Holy Spirit works in the heart of every man and therefore in every religion. We certainly have to understand verses 9 to 12 in a very liberal sense. They concern the extensive action of the Word both before and after the Incarnation. Finally, the text concludes: 'He came among his own and his own knew him not'. I do not think that we have to restrict this term 'his own' to the people of Israel, for what is in question is the Word who enlightens every man that comes into this world. His own did not receive him, but some people did receive him. 'But to all those who have received him he has given the power to become children of God'. These verses seem to have a very wide reference and to pose the problem of the divine sonhood of all men.

All those who have received the Word are to become children of God. In addition, this sonhood was already one of the characteristics of the religion of Israel, and we cannot restrict it to those who acknowledge the incarnate Word. Sonhood through participation in the unique sonhood of Christ is therefore a completion of the sonhood offered to every man who has received the Word of God.

Moreover, in accordance with a very old tradition, the Word has always been at work in those who are looking for God.

SALVATION IN RELIGIONS AND SALVATION IN CHRIST

The very practical question which now arises is that of the value of various religions in ensuring the salvation of their adherents. The question is often asked in a rather simplistic manner: 'Is it because of their religion or in spite of it that non-Christians can be saved?'

First we must say clearly that no one is properly speaking 'saved' by his religion. A religion is only the location or framework within which a mysterious grace goes to work; or, more simply, forces which are both human and divine. Therefore we have to distinguish the forces which take effect from the ways in which we use, imagine and present them in a theological doctrine.

The forces present here all arise from the same thrust of human life in search of its chief end, and its realization in a better 'world'. This force, which comes from God, cannot take effect without the impulse, aid and attraction of divine power. That is the essential thing and that will remain when all the superstructures have disappeared.

Therefore I am confronted with a profound life which is responsible for everything that I am and the divine life which is offered to me both in my very own nature and in Jesus the Christ. This divine life is something that men have tried to grasp. Feeling its action within them they have given it a countenance, a shape and a structure. From that basis the religions were born, with all their doctrinal, theological, liturgical and other devices.

The same forces take effect in all religions, but, I should say, with differing degrees of intensity. In accordance with Christ's own words, it would seem that in faith in Christ we have access to more intimate sharing in that power or force of life which he is always telling us about. The Incarnation gave us the possibility of drawing more deeply from the very well-springs of life because in Christ we are children of God in a more intimate way. In Christ the divine life is offered to us in a way more intense than hitherto. At the same time that this life is given to us in abundance, Christ's revelation allows us a deeper apprehension of the mystery of God. Hence the coming of Christ and his reception increase both the divine life and illumination within us.

In every man's heart, even before and apart from any knowledge of Christ, it is always the life of God which is communicated by his Word and his Spirit. It is therefore the same life which takes effect in a Buddhist or in a Hindu. To be sure, they represent this life as it passes by way of Buddha, or Vishnu, or Shiva, or others. They offer no explicit recognition of Christ, but it is Christ who is active in them as the Word of God and this 'action' is offered to them within the framework of their religion. It is important here to remember that Christ 'belongs' to Christianity and that the Word of God belongs to all men.

We may say, then, that these believers are saved in their own religion, for effectively it is within this context and within this framework that divine grace takes effect. We may say that they are saved 'by' their religion, for it is for them the actual means, and the location and agency of divine grace. No religion is of itself the ultimate cause of salvation. What 'causes' salvation for someone is his adherence to the divine grace operating in each religion, or rather in each believer. Though we may say that each religion is an actual means of salvation, it is still the Word of God that remains the definitive Saviour of mankind.

But that does not mean that all religions have the same objective capacity of putting us in contact with divine grace. Not all offer their believers the same possibility of contact with the divine. On this point we have to be realistic and not to try to put everything on the same level or reduce everything to the same scale. If Christ tells us that he is the way, the truth and the life, we may conclude that we have through him a deeper, more direct and real means of access than we would have if we followed a master who only showed us the way. It is here precisely that Christ brings us a unique testimony, through his relation to the Father. It is on this oneness of person and message that the claims of Christianity are founded—and those were also Christ's claims before they became those of his Church. This amounts to saying that the Word incarnate offers us in his person, in Christianity, a more actual, more explicit and richer way of salvation than he offers to any man in the other religions. It is difficult to interpret in any other way the mystery of the Incarnation and of the Church. These claims may seem exorbitant, but if Christ really is what he tells us he is, the unique and personal manifestation of the Father, then we have to accept the consequences.

<h2 style="text-align:center">CONSEQUENCES FOR EVANGELIZATION</h2>

The Gospel is both universal and singular, like Christ himself. In choosing the Incarnation as the means of salvation for the world, God opted for the particular. Christ was a man born of woman, in a small nation, and so on. He was a Jew and very much a Jew. This is the extreme aspect of the singular case. But in making himself man, the Word of God did not merely take on one particular human nature; he also assumed a universal human nature. This human nature has to be seen, as in the Chinese tradition, as a reality and not as a concept. In fact, in taking on human nature, the Word became just as much 'any man' as he is 'a' man. The Incarnation affected all mankind to this degree of depth of nature. Perhaps the West no longer sees very clearly what human nature can be, but in eastern Asia the problem of nature is fundamental and comes before that of personality or person. If we allow of this profound community of nature, the relation between Christ and Adam becomes properly meaningful and original sin no longer seems incomprehensible.

This return to ontology is absolutely necessary if we want to understand what salvation in Christ can mean for people who have never heard of him. Why should we not believe that all humanity was affected by the Incarnation? In what way? It is difficult to say. But we may interpret the words of Paul in this sense when he says that since we have all sinned in Adam, we have all found salvation in Christ. Surely it was this mysterious action of Christ in every man, taking effect through his Incarnation, at the very level of human nature, which enabled evangelization to be seen as a response to a profound expectation on the part of man? The proclamation of Christ's word is capable of awakening a response in the heart of every man who really wants to hear it.

But here we have the objection that if that is the case, if any man can be saved, and if grace is at work in the heart of human nature, why should we wish to evangelize that nature? The reply is to be found only in God's own attitude. He had to make himself one of us, and had to do so for all mankind; but for some time there was no urgency. That is why he came at a relatively late date, in our sense at least, in the history of mankind. Then each nation already had its patriarchs and its prophets.

When Christ came among us, he did not emerge in all directions, as it were, as if he had no time to lose. He had a lot of time to lose. He never behaved as if he thought that the salvation of the world depended on his activity. He was not a fanatic obsessed with the need to do something. And yet he knew that he was bringing salvation. He was to bring it and in a very real sense he was to represent it as already realized.

Perhaps this freedom of Christ is something that we have to redis-cover. We have to be convinced, as Christ was, that he brings us something new and something very new. In Christ we have greater access to the divine life and we know through him things that he alone could tell us about God, because he came from God and because he is God himself. In this superabundance, this liberality of giving, we find the justification of evangelization. It enters into the dynamics of revela-tion. It is the proclamation of the hidden mystery which Paul speaks of in his letter to the Ephesians (Eph 3: 1-13) and in Colossians (Col 1: 24-29).

Just as the Gospel will not necessarily convince those who hear it, so its proclamation will very often have the effect of reawakening its hearers' faith in their own religion. It can even happen that we cannot openly put forward the Christian message, and all we can do is to encourage those who listen to us to deepen their own religion, so that they find there the spiritual light of their existence. Then we are like travellers who travel as it were together, in one another's company, yet apart, each on his own pathway. We have two things in common: the same Word of God that awakens and attracts us, more or less clearly and explicitly. All of us are searching. It is not the fact of knowing Christ that entitles us to say or to believe that we have reached the goal. We travel in Jesus Christ, but Christ will always be a mystery. In this humble attitude that we can share with the faithful of all religions, we proclaim the Gospel and we hope that one day, God knows when, we shall all recognize in Jesus of Nazareth the Word of God who has always been present and active in the heart of all men and of all reli-gions.

Translated by John Griffiths

Norbert Mette

Evangelization and the Credibility of the Church

THE CONNECTION BETWEEN EVANGELIZATION AND CREDIBILITY

THE apostolic exhortatio *Evangelii nuntiandi* of 1975 insisted that
'evangelization' must not be thought of as just a subdivision of
ecclesiastical activity. By stressing that the fundamental importance of
the concept leads us back to the basis of all Church activity, this
document was also a clear reminder of how closely evangelization and
the credibility of the Church are intertwined. It is not enough to suppose that the Church can only become credible when the Gospel becomes the sole standard of its actual life and activity. Of course this
only comes about when the Church engages in evangelization. We can
even say that *the more seriously the Church takes the task of evangelization, the more credible it becomes.* The reason is simple. A Church
which evangelizes very soon realizes that it will only succeed in
preaching the Gospel of Jesus Christ to the world credibly if it bears
witness to that Gospel, not only in its words but in its ordinary practice. On the other hand, we find again and again that a Church which
neglects the task of evangelization is very soon in danger of losing sight
of this connection. The Church then becomes an end in itself; it becomes more interested in improving its own situation than in improving
the human situation.

There is no need to go back to the history of the Church to find
specific examples of this connection between evangelization and the
Church's credibility. The present situation of the Church is in itself an
impressive demonstration of this. To oversimplify a little, it is the

Churches in the Third World, in the areas the Church has traditionally regarded as 'mission territories', which currently seem to many to bear convincing witness to the Gospel and are consequently the source of great hopes.

In contrast, the Churches in the traditionally Christian countries, taken as a whole, are clearly suffering a rapid loss of credibility. Fewer and fewer people can see how the life and teaching of these Churches is to be reconciled with the message of the Gospel. One is forced to ask whether this is not connected in some way with the different degree of commitment to evangelization observable in these Churches? Is the real reason for this difference in the credibility of the Churches perhaps that one Church presents the picture of a Church in which anxious concern about its own preservation and perpetuation is the main emotion and in which all energies are concentrated on preserving past gains, whereas the other Church, with some justification, gives the impression that in it the Gospel's concern with a total renewal of the whole human race—and not just of the Church—is genuinely and consistently taken seriously?

If we look at the total commitment of the Churches of the Third World to the *service of the Gospel,* we see at once how much *concern for the institution* dominates the Churches of the western countries. This comparative consideration allows us to draw the following picture of the profiles of the two churches, which gains in vividness what it loses by oversimplification.[1] On the one hand is a Church so absorbed in its internal problems that it has hardly any strength left for missionary commitment and is therefore arousing less and less interest. On the other is a Church which, precisely because it feels an involvement in the actual sufferings and aspirations of mankind and tries to give real expression to the message of God's coming to take up his rule by joining in the struggle to achieve a decent life for all, has learnt to neglect its own interests and is thereby increasing in credibility. And if we want to learn more about the reasons for this lack of credibility of the Church on the one hand and the way new credibility can be won on the other, there is no need to go into abstract theorizing. It is enough to look at and analyze the differences in practice.

'INSTITUTIONALISM' AS A CRISIS OF EVANGELIZATION

Even if the crisis affecting the Churches in the western countries cannot be attributed exclusively to it,[2] there is no denying that their own behaviour is clearly a contributory factor. The Churches are giving more and more people the impression of being more concerned about themselves than the Gospel, and this impression seems by now so firmly rooted that mere apologetics can no longer eliminate it. Instead of rejecting it, we must ask whether there really is no basis at all for this feeling of unease? Are not the Churches in these countries more and more taking on the appearance of an institution so concerned with itself that it can hardly see other problems? Where do these Churches really display the 'characteristics of a community of hope'? Rather than being somewhere where new experiences of human contact can be found, the life of the Church seems to be dominated by the same social pressures and mechanisms as all other areas of society.[3]

Nothing shows more clearly how important the concern with the institution has become in these Churches, how far their thought and action is concentrated on keeping themselves going, than the recent massive expansion of the Church's administrative apparatus. In some cases this has gone so far that the growth in the administration bears almost no relation to the tasks these Churches now have to perform. Can we blame people for being unable to reconcile this lavish bureaucracy with the Church's primary function of service, or for being disappointed in their expectations that the Church would prove to be a defender of humanness in its own activities?

I have no intention of claiming that the Church irrevocably betrays its task of evangelization immediately it concerns itself with the expansion of its institution, but what is important is that the two should be kept in a certain proportion. If this is not done it is easy for the Church's efforts to give the presence of the Gospel in a society a firm base, institutional as well as personal, to produce precisely the opposite effect to that intended. There are signs of such an ominous development in the Churches in the western countries. There is no getting away from it: for all the extension of their organization they are on the road to stagnation. Their growing institutional presence in society is matched by a declining missionary impact. Not only are they scarcely capable any longer of winning new convinced members; even within their own ranks the chances of transmitting the faith are becoming increasingly precarious. The churches are becoming less and less capable of impressing the contents of the Christian faith on the minds of the next generation.[4]

Not that the person of Jesus and the Gospel encounter total rejection. On the contrary, their attraction is still extraordinarily great, and the Gospel still helps to guide the lives of many people. However, fewer and fewer people can reconcile the appeal which comes from the Christian message with their experience of the Church. Their experience of the Church is of an institution more obsessed with the acceptance of certain structures and laws than interested in the possibilities for action contained in the Gospel. They accuse the Church of being interested mainly in its own security as an institution. In their eyes this sterile narrowness stifles a practice of love based on the goal of universal solidarity contained in the Christian message. And it makes sense. A Church which gives the impression of being mainly concerned with the most efficient possible administration of vestiges of the past is not a likely source of ideas about the future, and so incapable of arousing great interest.

It is, however, not purely accidental that concern with the institution is currently so important in the Churches of the West, nor, for the same reason, can the situation be corrected simply by a fundamentalist return to the Gospel. What seems to be at work here is much more the current peak of an intellectual tradition in the Church in which Christianity is absorbed into the institutional Church, and for which therefore a stress on the institutional Church and all the efforts to expand it and increase its area of influence do not derive from some obsession with power but are seen as the appropriate form for evangelization.[5] In practice, as is becoming increasingly clear, such an identification of Christianity and the Church, of Gospel and institution, has extremely dangerous consequences. One of these is that only what can be defined and organized by the official institution counts as an action of the Christian Church. People become objects of the Church's care, and for them to work out their own interpretations of the faith or their own forms of ecclesial community is impossible.

There is no need here for a detailed description of the extent to which this 'institutionalist' view of the Church has left its mark on both the theory and the practice of missionary activity.[6] The traditional mission reflected this mentality in its very structures, and there are many indications that this too is the source of the crisis of mission.[7] The Churches in the Third World seem more prepared ruthlessly to expose these connections between the 'institutionalist' view of the Church and the crisis of evangelization and to draw the appropriate conclusions. Surrounded by the growing evidence of their own crisis, the Churches in the western countries can therefore learn from them what urgent changes must be made in both Church activity and theological theory if they are to win new credibility.

EVANGELIZATION AS THE BASIS OF THE CHURCH'S CREDIBILITY

'Churches in the Third World' here means those Christian or ecclesial movements which have freed themselves from the tutelage of the Churches of the West and in their activity are setting out on new paths in an attempt to take account of their particular situation.[8] It is characteristic of the new approach of these churches that it starts from a radical return to treating evangelization as the basic function of the Church. The result is that these Churches no longer let themselves be dominated by an 'institutionalist' view, but are learning to see the world and themselves in terms of evangelization. In the process, concern with the Church, in so far as it is concerned with the interests of group egoism, becomes less and less important. It is replaced by the much greater worry of how the Church can really succeed in bearing credible witness to the Gospel in its words and actions. That under some circumstances this can involve disadvantages for it as an institution is clearly realized by the Churches in the Third World. How sharply they have broken with the traditional 'institutionalism' in their thinking and action can be illustrated by looking at three of their most characteristic features.

1. The Churches in the Third World are becoming increasingly aware of the disastrous consequences of a 'mission' which, in its zeal for the salvation of souls and its efforts to establish the Church among all nations, was conceived without regard for any real situation. This made it all the easier for the mission to become a tool of outside interests, which ultimately led these Churches into an abnormally heavy dependence on a particular socio-cultural situation. To extricate themselves from these ties they must do more than consider the internal problems of the Church. For them, awareness of the context, a thorough analysis of the situation of their societies, is therefore an elementary precondition for the performance of their task. This is the only way to prevent the misuse of the Gospel by rulers as a means of keeping people happy. It is the only way of ensuring that Christian action has a genuinely liberating effect in the actual situation.

2. The Churches in the Third World are coming increasingly to see it as an authentic Christian responsibility to act on behalf of those 'who cannot yet speak for themselves, to whom nobody would listen and for whom nobody else will speak',[9] the weak and those who have no rights, the poor and oppressed. They know that the credibility of the Gospel is under greater threat from the situation of these 'unpersons' (G. Gutiérrez) than it could ever be from intellectual doubts. Faced with this situation, the Church cannot afford to try and please everyone, to get everyone's applause. What is required here is to take sides firmly, even if the result is social disapproval. The Churches in the Third World are demonstrating what it means to let the authenticity of 'the good news for the poor' lead them away from any form of pure self-assertion to live and work in total solidarity 'with those who cannot help themselves and to stand with them in their struggle for liberation'.[10]

3. If one feature is characteristic of the Churches in the Third World,

it is 'the formation of basic communities of the most varied kinds, which draw their understanding of the faith and of the Church from their own situation and avoid the pressure of rigid ecclesiastical institutions'.[11] This too is a direct consequence of the way these churches take the task of evangelization seriously. The Gospel, after all, is not simply addressed to individuals; it is only experienced as the good news where it brings people together, forms them into groups, where it inspires new forms of rich community. The basic communities allow the Church to be experienced as a 'community of hope' in a very immediate and convincing way. They give 'the Christian faith life and the power to give meaning and direction to the individual's life'.[12]

In these groups the shared experience of being a Christian produces a refreshing spontaneity. Instead of waiting for instructions from above, they put the Gospel into practice as they think right, though without setting their practice up as an absolute. In this way they create a Church which is built up 'from below' rather than being simply administered 'from on top'. Naturally it should not be overlooked that the financial position of these Churches does not allow them to develop such a rigid administrative structure as some western Churches. The advantage, on the other hand, is obvious: they do not need to get involved in legal and organizational details, and so find it much easier to win authority by virtue of 'religious competence' (J.B. Metz).[13]

The Churches in the Third World do not use the latest techniques of public relations to improve their image, but prefer to rely on the Gospel. The lesson is clear: evangelization is all that is needed for credibility.

Notes

1. It must of course be remembered that the churches of the western world are still to some extent present in the Third World, just as the Church of the Third World is influencing a growing number of groups within the western Churches.

2. Cf. for example 'Kirche in der Krise', *Concilium* 12 (1976), vol. 4.

3. Cf. 'Unsere Hoffnung', statement by the Joint Synod of the Dioceses of West Germany, vol. I (Freiburg, 1976), pp. 84-111, esp. 99-100.

4. This was one of the main findings of a survey among German Catholics; cf., F.-X. Kaufmann, 'Empirische Sozialforschung zwischen Soziologie und Theologie', in: K. Forster, ed., *Befragte Katholiken—Zur Zukunft von Glaube und Kirche* (Freiburg, 1973), pp. 185-97, esp., p. 191. Similarly, K. Rahner, *Strukturwandel der Kirche als Aufgabe und Chance* (Freiburg, 1972).

5. In the Catholic Church the origins of this tradition are in Counter-Reformation ecclesiology, and it reached a peak at the First Vatican Council, which cited the Church in its institutional form as a motive for belief. Cf. DS, 3031ff.

6. Cf. L. Rutti, 'Mission—Gegenstand der Praktischen Theologie oder Frage an die Gesamttheologie? Überlegungen zum Ende der kolonialen Mission', in: F. Klostermann & R. Zerfass, eds., *Praktische Theologie heute* (Munich, 1974), pp. 288-307.

7. Cf., ibid., pp. 296ff.

8. Cf., esp. 'Die Kirchen in der Dritten Welt und ihre theologische Aufgabe', Memorandum of the Ecumenical Consultation in Dar-es-Salaam, 5-12 August 1976, in: *Ökumenische Rundschau* 26 (1977), pp. 211-23.

9. Bensberger Kreis, ' "Offene Gemeinde", Memorandum deutscher Katholiken', *Concilium* 11 (1975), pp. 289-95, esp. 294.

10. 'Die Kirchen in der Dritten Welt' (see above, n. 8), p. 222.

11. L. Rutti, op. cit., in n. 6, p. 299.

12. Bensberger Kreis, art. cit. in n. 9, p. 294.

13. Cf. J.B. Metz, *Followers of Christ* (London & New York, 1978), pp. 60ff.

Duraisamy Amalorpavadass

Evangelization and Culture

THE RELATIONSHIP and mutual influence between the Gospel and culture is a difficult matter and a perennial problem. It has become a burning issue with the process of decolonization and attainment of political independence by many African and Asian countries and the consequent renaissance of indigenous cultures. The theological discussion that followed became vigorous at Vatican II. The debate reached its climax and the implications were articulated at the Synod of Bishops in 1974. This came in the wake of an original understanding of the local church and its essential mission of evangelization.

A DILEMMA BETWEEN TWO CONCERNS: RELATION OF CULTURE AND RELIGION

The problem has been often evaded by playing one of two dangers against the other. On the one hand, Christianity has projected a bad image of itself in the course of its missionary enterprise during the last five centuries. The acceptance of the Gospel and the expression of Christian faith meant that the converts and the young Churches of these countries should also adopt the culture of the missionaries and the mission Churches. Christianization meant westernization in terms of socio-cultural life. It contributed to the disparaging of local cultures of the people evangelized, their alienation from their social milieus and religious traditions, their evasion of their countries' historical adventure, and their drifting away from the mainstream of national life. On the other hand, one feared that if the Church assimilated even the values, good elements and inspiring practices of other religions it might be absorbed by the culture and religion of the place and thereby lose its identity. Enculturation was viewed with caution and suspicion. One was advised to preach a 'pure, simple, neutral Gospel', a Gospel deprived of all socio-cultural expressions. What was considered 'pure', 'simple', 'neutral' and 'safe' was in fact a socio-cultural expression of the West. While so doing, one was engaged in another form of enculturation, through unawareness, namely imposing upon the evangelized people a western cultural form of Christianity. Even today some shirk indigenization on the understanding that there is no connection between culture and religion, or by identifying western Christianity with universality.

Theoretically one professed to steer clear of the two possible dangers. In fact people did make a choice, and alienated the members of the young Churches. This alienation was so strong that one generation after the departure of the colonial masters and the transfer of Church leadership to the local leaders, much of the Third World is by and large hostile to any effort of indigenization.

Culture and religion are two separate entities with identities of their own. Yet both are living realities connected with people. Their vitality consists in their openness to other realities and to growth and dynamic synthesis, by a continuous process of acceptance of some elements and rejection of others and in the awareness of their respective identities. Hence the first condition for a genuine enculturation is to be aware of and to admit the interaction and reciprocal influence between culture and religion. Culture influences religion; religion influences culture. Now this mutual openness and influence are not at all a threat to their identity, just as two persons, mature and adult, can enrich themselves by friendly sharing and yet maintain their personal identities. While one's identity should by all means be preserved, false identities should be shed. Christianity has no identity except the spirit of Jesus Christ and the sign of fraternal love patterned on Christ's own love, to the point of dying for others (Jn 13:35). The rest is only a cultural identity which is derived from a particular society and which should be shed in view of a new enculturation in a new milieu. In this understanding we have to see clearly whether enculturation is a constitutive element of the mission of the Church. If so, what is the process of an authentic enculturation? What is the theological basis for it? What are its practical implications?

CONDITIONS OF AN AUTHENTIC ENCULTURATION

Enculturation follows the incarnation of the Word, and the constitution of the Church

The incarnation of the Word determines the nature of the Church (*Lumen Gentium* 8). If so, the choice is not between indigenization and non-indigenization, but between being an authenic Church of Christ and not being a Church at all. So the Church expresses itself, in its being and action, through an incarnational procedure (*Ad Gentes*, 10 s.). In the present dispensation, which is an incarnational economy, the humanity of Christ is the visible sign, efficacious instrument, and permanent agency of the Word in his work of salvation. Likewise the Spirit of Jesus, dead and risen, becomes manifest as active presence and transforming power in the visible community of Christ's disciples. The Gospel becomes the power of God for salvation of all who believe (Rom. 1:16) through words, deeds, signs and wonders, in the history of the world, in the life of the Church, and in the culture of a people. The values of this Gospel or the reality of the new era are to be translated and communicated to others by the very life and activity of the Church through visible structures, community dimension, lived experience and concrete manifestations of life in various activities. The living Gospel lived by the Church in a living culture with all the transformations it entails is what is called enculturation. Hence there is no preaching of the Gospel without enculturation.

While this is accepted in theory, some find it difficult to commit themselves to indigenization at the level of praxis. Some understand incarnation in a static manner. It is the most dynamic and most personal encounter between God and man in the very dynamics of human existence and world history. It also set in a dynamic process a transformation in each man, in the whole human community and in the whole cosmos.

Enculturation realizes universality and overcomes particularities of all sorts

Some fear and oppose indigenization as a tendency towards division and nationalism and as a potential danger to the universality of the Church. This is obviously a fear on the part of those who have been used to think of the universal Church as something abstract, who consider uniformity as the means of unity, and who attribute authenticity and loyalty to what conforms to a particular cultural model. In reality, universality can only be realized through particularities, unity only through variety, and authenticity through originality. This particularity of incarnation was the guarantee of the authenticity of Christ's total identification with man and served as the means for realizing the universality of his mission. Likewise the Church has to be localized in order to be visible and universal. And in each particular Church the full and universal Church is present. In the same way, enculturation necessarily supposes particular cultural expressions in all domains; but universality and unity are realized by the one Spirit, by the same faith and by communion in the values of the Gospel. Universality cannot be realized by spreading a single particularity that imposes a particular cultural expression on all peoples and on all cultures.

Enculturation to be in continuity with the healthy and venerable tradition of the Church and in discontinuity with its recent ambiguous tradition

The opponents of enculturation wonder what is wrong with the present Church and its expressions. They plead that this has been handed on by a tradition which is after all four centuries old.

One should respect tradition. Tradition is nothing less than the life of the Church under the guidance of the Spirit and with the leadership of the magisterium. Yet everything in tradition is not of the same value.

Holiness and sin, fidelity and infidelity could co-exist in the Church. Likewise one period or one section of the Church could be more faithful to Christ and the Gospel than others. Respect for tradition also involves a critique and discernment.

The effort to indigenize the Church today is very much in continuity with a longer, more ancient and venerable tradition that can be traced back to Jesus Christ, the Word incarnate himself. When the Word was made flesh, he identified himself fully with the Jewish people, spoke their language (Aramaic), followed their customs and tradition, and was involved in the life of his society. The first Christian community, formed of converts from Judaism, retained some of their religious traditions, practices and prayer forms. When the Gospel penetrated into the Graeco-Roman societies, Greek and Latin and socio-cultural signs were integrated into the liturgy. The theology of the Church was elaborated on the Graeco-Roman modes of thought. A similar process took place when the Gospel spread to East Syria, Egypt and countries of northern Europe. Their languages and cultures, signs and symbols, customs and practices were adopted. New original and authentic forms of liturgy, theology and spirituality were evolved. A similar process was evident when the slaves were evangelized in eastern Europe. The best example of in-depth and all-round enculturation was the transformation which took place in the culture of western Europe.

In these and in all other instances the spirit of the Gospel permeated the cultures of the place, transformed them profoundly, and enriched them. It also gave them a new dynamism for growth, new meaning and orientation.

When the new worlds of America, Asia and Africa were discovered, the original principle of incarnation and the traditional process of indigenization were not followed. Instead of announcing the Gospel to the new peoples in such a way as to facilitate the emergence of new spontaneous, new creative expressions in those societies, missionaries spread the already developed western cultural expressions of the Gospel they were used to in their home countries. This approach and practice prevented a normal enculturation process in the new areas.

Vatican II, far from teaching a new doctrine and initiating a new tradition, reaffirmed the age-old Christian principle of incarnation; in so doing, it relaunched the process of enculturation and enabled the earlier and authentic Christian tradition to continue in spite of the break of four centuries.

Enculturation brings about not one universal Christian culture, but many particular Christian cultures

A myth that is often spread in order to oppose enculturation consists in stating that after all we have *the* Christian culture and there is no need for us to take things from secular culture or any other religious culture.

'The Christian culture' one refers to and in which one takes pride is the particular Christian culture of western Europe or of America, not in its modern or latest form but in anachronistic and decadent forms. Instead we should speak of many 'Christian cultures'. That is to say, the indigenous culture of every country and region must be permeated by the spirit of the Gospel, purified, enriched and fulfilled by Gospel values and the spirit of Christ. There could be as many Christian cultures as there are cultures in the world. It is fitting that Christians of these countries should learn from and appreciate the values of their Christian inheritance from the West; but they should also be aware and proud of their indigenous cultures which are, in some sense, Christian since the Word of God has been at work in them (*Ad Gentes*, 18).

Enculturation covers the total reality of the Church

Indigenization is concerned with every aspect of the Church's life and with every sector of its activity. Indigenous expressions refer to the formation of the local community of Christians and training of the clergy and the religious, to their life-style or sociological adaptation, to the incarnation of the Gospel in actual life situations and in every sphere of personal and family life, social and civic activities, to economic and political systems and the cultures of each country; to theology, spirituality, the triple ministries of the word (preaching, evangelization, catechesis), worship (liturgy) and service (formation and organization of Christian community towards Christian maturity, witness in society and humble service in love). There is a connection among all of them. *Ad Gentes* outlines a whole gamut of programmes to be covered by enculturation (22,18). There is no order in which the process should be initiated. Each person or group or Church could start from one aspect according to circumstances, needs, and resources, and from here, under the dynamism of commitment to the cause, could proceed to cover the other aspects and dimensions.

Indigenization should embrace the three dimensions of history

In the mind of some, enculturation connotes a return to the ancient culture of the people, a mere revival of their irrelevant past and a going backwards, while each country is moving forwards to shape its future. Some wonder why the Church should adapt itself to a culture whose values are being thrown overboard by the 'westernized *élite*' and where the values of modern technological culture are avidly swallowed. Others wonder whether the Church should incarnate herself in the national or local culture of a people while modern culture is sweeping across the whole world submerging local cultures. Others say: Culture is in the melting pot; let us wait for the period of stability.

We witness today not only a spread of international culture but the renaissance of national cultures. The identity of a national culture and an experience of it are necessary for one's own national personality as well as for the ability to relate oneself with other national cultures and to participate meaningfully in a world culture. Culture as a living and dynamic reality will always be in continuous evolution and can never come to a state of stability; hence enculturation cannot wait till then. In the same way indigenization should address itself to both ancient and modern cultures in so far as the values, elements and aspects of the ancient culture continue to be in vogue today and permeate the modern form of one's national culture. The present may have its roots in the past, its dynamic orientation may be towards the future, but the Church is indigenous in so far as it is relevantly present to the actual reality.

Finally, within the same country or region or place there are various cultures. In such a situation, enculturation does not mean a single uniform expression for the whole country, but a variety of forms. Yet one cannot fail to recognize a basic core or dynamic unity underlying and interconnecting all of them.

Mission and indigenization are simultaneous and not successive

In the past many were, and even today many still are, under the impression that in an initial stage the word is simply announced, celebrated and lived, and it is at a later stage that all these activities are to

be adapted to a country and integrated in its culture; first evangelization and then enculturation; first liturgy as celebrated in the culture of
the missionary, and then adaptation to the mission country, and so on.
But in reality both are so intimately connected that they should constitute a whole and should be carried out simultaneously.

Enculturation includes religious traditions as part of the total reality

Some agree to enculturation but limit its scope to culture and will not
extend it to religious realities. This is expressed, for instance, in India
by saying: 'Indianization—yes; but Hinduization—No'. It is difficult to
find a culture completely impervious to religion, or to keep a religion
unaffected by culture. In Asian countries for instance, all cultures are
both secular and religious. It is Hinduism that has predominantly,
though not exclusively, shaped the Indian culture and therefore enculturation in India involves incarnation chiefly in Hindu culture.

A global understanding of creation, redemptive incarnation and the
Church's universal mission will help us to overcome any limitation of
the scope of enculturation. The whole of creation is the effective manifestation of God's Word: (Jn 1:12; Col 15-17). The same Word has
been present throughout human history revealing himself in various
ways to various peoples. The seeds of the Word (*Ad Gentes*) are found
in all religious and temporal realities. The plan of God was to bring
everything together under Christ as head (Eph 1:9-10). Through incarnation he assumes the whole creation in order to redeem and unify it.
Nothing is saved unless it is assumed; and everything that has been
created must be saved (II Cor 5:17-21, Eph 2:11-22, Col 1:15-20).
Now this recapitulation in Christ includes not only the salvation of
souls, but that of the whole man and all men, not only men but all that
is human, not only cultures but religions, all that is religious and cultural; in short, all creation (Rom 8:18-23). By his death and resurrection Christ became the Lord of the universe and saviour of mankind.
His spirit fills the universe. We have no right to exclude anything—
especially religions—from the object of salvation and enculturation;
'we cannot call profane what God has made clean' (Acts 10:15, 45). If
so, the religions are not outside but take their place within God's one
plan of salvation centred in Christ. Wherever truth, goodness, beauty,
purity and holiness are found they originate in God and belong to God.
They should be recognized as the inheritance of Christ (Ps 2:6; Col
1:20). The Church has to gather into unity and consecrate to God
through Christ the whole of creation and humankind. She cannot dis-
own them as alien. Everything belongs to us, we belong to Christ, and

Christ himself belongs to God (I Cor 3:23), so that God may be all in all. Hence the Church should acknowledge, preserve and promote 'the spiritual and moral goods found among these men, as well as the values in their society and culture' (*Nostra Aetate 2*, cfr. *Ad Gentes* 11,9,22). With this clear statement and teaching of Vatican II none can say that elements from religions cannot be integrated into Christian theology, worship, prayer life and spirituality, provided of course they can all be Christianized. Enculturation includes, in this correct sense, some kind of Hinduization in India.

Enculturation realizes the Church's catholicity and fulness

Many do not consider enculturation useful or even necessary, since the Church is the universal sacrament of salvation and has the fulness of revelation in Christ, and therefore possesses all the other religions.

Even though Christ is the total, ultimate and definite revelation of God, and even though this Christ is present in the Church, one cannot identify Christ with the Church. Nor can one limit his presence and gift to the Church alone. The one true Church founded by Christ subsists in the Catholic Church (*Lumen Gentium* 8) but is not exhausted by it. The Church is the sign and instrument of salvation for all men. Yet salvation is also possible under certain conditions for those not visibly integrated with the Catholic Church (*Lumen Gentium* 16). The Church has truth and goodness, grace and salvation, but it cannot exhaust them; it does not have a monopoly of them. The kingdom is present in the Church, but they are not identical. Like every other sign, it is less than the reality. That is why the Church tends, in continuous pilgrimage, towards fulness (*Lumen Gentium* 8).

By evangelization and enculturation the dynamism of the Church towards its catholicity is made operative and effective. At the same time the elements outside it want to be integrated into the Catholic fellowship and unity. So Vatican II asks the Church to realize its insufficiency and to borrow from other religions with the least possible hesitation, shame and complex (*Ad Gentes* 22). In this sense, the prophecy of Isaiah is fully applicable to the Church: 'To this people it was said in prophecy: enlarge the space of your tent, spread out your tent cloths unsparingly' (Is 54, 2. cf. *Ad Gentes* 9).

Enculturation supposes participation in the paschal mystery

Enculturation calls for a prophetic critique and a Christic interpretation. Enculturation is based on the mystery of incarnation, but it is redemptive. Enculturation recognizes the presence of evil in the world, the reality of sin and its imprints, forces and consequences in all realities of the world and human life. The Church should continue to live the paschal mystery in its life and mission as a continuing reality. The process of redemptive incarnation or participation in the paschal mystery comprises three stages: (*a*) incarnation: presence to and assumption of everything and everybody; (*b*) death: destroying hostility, putting to death the body of sin, liberating men and all realities from sin, error, superstition, corruption and death; (*c*) resurrection and glorification: salvation in Christ is not only a liberation from sin but positively the realization of a new creation, leading a new kind of human existence, having a deeper and fuller unity, and realizing fulfillment in wholeness and harmony.

This holds good for enculturation. One should not indiscriminately admit anything and everything from the doctrines and practices of religions into the liturgy, theology or spirituality, and so on; nor can one assume them as they are. They should be first brought to the touchstone of Christ. They should be first made to pass through his death and resurrection. They should be subjected to Christian critique. Any authentic enculturation will reject false doctrines, superstition, all forms of sin and evil: in short, whatever cannot be Christianized. Nothing can be adopted unless it has values, unless it acquires a Christian meaning through a Christian interpretation; unless it is oriented towards a Christian goal, under the guidance of the Spirit (*Ad Gentes* 8, 11).

Enculturation should include the liturgy

Some will grant indigenization of everything except the liturgy. This is due to the understanding that the liturgy is a water-tight compartment; that it is sacred while the rest is profane. If liturgy is the supreme manifestation of the mystery of the Church and the most efficacious means of fulfilling her mission, if it is the fount and the summit of all its activities (*Sacrosanctum Concilium* 10), mission and enculturation which are carried out throughout the day in various spheres should reach their culmination in the celebration of the liturgy in indigenous forms. That is why the Council has given us norms for liturgical enculturation (*Sacrosanctum Concilium* 37-40).

Enculturation implies creativity and originality, dynamism and relevance

If the local Church is considered as only a part of the universal Church and as a lower administrative unit, the attitude of the former will be one of importing and copying, of merely implementing orders and conforming to what comes from the top, in passive receptivity. There will be uniformity and sameness everywhere; but it will be irrelevant and cease to be a Church. On the contrary, if every local Church contains the full mystery of the Church and expresses itself in its socio-cultural milieu, then there will be creativity and originality. It is high time that the young Churches started being themselves. The variety and changing character of reality calls for and necessitates pastoral pluralism, starting from cultural, ecclesial and theological pluralism. It will have to take the initiative, become competent and responsible, have the imagination and daring to invent relevant forms and patterns, structures and institutions for its various activities and services. This calls for a correct understanding of the relationship between the universal Church and the particular Churches. The administrative system of the Churches has to be very much decentralized and the principle of subsidiarity must be followed to its last exigencies and implications.

Enculturation is community responsibility and concerted action

If the Church's mystery is expressed and its mission fulfilled through enculturation it follows that the community character of the Church should shine out in the total process and at every stage. It is not a random effort of some enthusiasts, nor a luxury reserved to some specialists. It is a community venture. It is inevitable that in the beginning only a small group will be convinced and be able to plan and execute things. Any movement has to start in a small way. Gradually it will grow. The rest of the people should be prepared for it by enlightenment and education. They should be consulted. They should have an initiation into the new forms of indigenization before changes are introduced into the Churches at any level. In this community effort, the leaders of the Church have a special and unique rôle to play. Their initiative and support, their official actions and personal example, will promote it (*Sacrosanctum Concilium*, 40; *Ad Gentes*, 22).

CONCLUSION

At the end of this practical theological reflection it seems appropriate to make a few remarks in order to link it up with what is taking place in many Churches of the Third World.

1. Even though a western form of Christianity was introduced into these countries, it is very difficult to assess the responsibility of missionary societies and individual missionaries. The theological understanding and political situation of their times were far from helpful. More enlightened individuals and groups did their best to follow a

different policy and to promote a limited programme of indigenization, but with little success. The missionaries of today have more than amply compensated for this by their efforts during the last two or three decades.

2. In spite of western cultural domination, indigenization has been realized in various degrees in some areas and aspects of the Church. So it would be wrong to state that the Churches of the Third World are totally western.

3. Against this background the indigenous leaders should accept their responsibility and play their rôle of leadership in the indigenization of the Church today, and forge ahead courageously with a well-planned programme. We have all the facilities and resources needed for such a task.

4. Enculturation, whether accepted or resisted, challenges our whole life. It is a process that affects our whole person, life and surroundings. If we accept it in some aspects, we become incongruous in the rest of our life. The effort that is demanded of us to convert ourselves and our life totally is formidable and long-drawn-out.

5. Yet it is a providential occasion offered to us to pass from a notion of the Church that is sectarian, static, introverted and imported to a notion that is catholic, dynamic, authentic, adult and creative.

6. The Church's mission should be understood as an all-round, ever-ready presence in various socio-cultural milieus through the Spirit of Christ. It is one of humble and loving service, and of losing a false identity in order to find a new identity which will be genuinely Christian and genuinely indigenous.

Marcello Zago

Evangelization in the
Religious Situation of Asia

THE 1974 SYNOD provided an occasion for reflection and writing on evangelization in the modern world. The interventions of the Asian bishops stressed, amongst other things, the subject of non-Christian religions, pointing to a new form of relationship in dialogue, a new method and form of evangelization, and a necessary way to acculturation.[1] Even if the new reality of secularizing societies and atheist regimes is a fact of life, evangelization in the religious sphere of Asian society still poses particular problems. The religious dimension in man, which opens him to the Absolute, and starts him out on a quest for total liberation, which has formed Asiatic peoples and cultures, and is still influential today even in the totalitarian regimes that profess atheism, always requires particular attention.

THE RELIGIOUS SITUATION IN ASIA

Many Asiatic countries still have religion as an integral part of their national culture, though it is banned or gravely restricted in some, and reduced to the personal sphere in others. There are three types of religion in Asia: the universalistic type originating outside the continent, such as Islam; the cultural-ethnic type such as Confucianism or Taoism in China, Shintoism in Japan and Hinduism in India; and the various types of animism spread more or less everywhere among minority ethnic groups. In this study I propose to deal only with religions of Asiatic origin, and therefore to leave Islam out of account.

Asiatic religions have one common characteristic, which can

perhaps be called tolerance toward other creeds, which allows for symbiosis or belonging to more than one tradition at the same time.[2] Religion is regarded rather as a way of experience and of life than as a monolithic whole, as a movement rather than as an obligatory structure. Buddhism, for example, admits an enormous number of degrees of adherence, within which groups of 'spirituals' or of monks provide the driving force. Its missionary endeavour is carried on above all by religious communities or 'masters of the spirit', who gradually come to influence their surroundings.

The Christian presence, after centuries of missionary effort, is numerically insignificant. Conversions have tended to take place among marginal animist groups or in countries without a great national religion, such as the Philippines; mass conversions have taken place only at times of socio-cultural crisis, as has happened in Korea, Vietnam and Taiwan in recent times, and in Sri-Lanka in the sixteenth century.[3]

Historically, the problem of the relationship between Christianity and the other great religions was seen by some great missionaries in the sixteenth and seventeenth centuries, but has yet to find a solution, due to inter-ecclesial polemics and disciplinary decisions,[4] and because of the theological bases and modes of thought of the whole of Christendom at that time. This failure to relate to other religions can be seen as one of the principal reasons for the disappointing results of missionary work.[5] Today, the theological presuppositions have changed, and the way is open for a more authentic encounter with other religions, in which direct evangelical witness will play a direct rôle.[6]

The lack of rapport with other religions, the fact that missionary presence and work are to be found almost exclusively outside the great currents of Asiatic culture, and a still low level of acculturation, together account for some particular difficulties in this situation. The Church appears as an alien entity, even to those Asians who perhaps know and love Christ;[7] it is a tree that fails to mature and bear fruit;[8] a philanthropic organization—so worthy of respect—rather than a way of spiritual experience.[9] Even though it everywhere uses local languages, there is a barrier to understanding in its religious language, even with regard to the ultimate Reality,[10] which makes even mutual understanding, let alone convincing the other side, difficult.

The methods used in the past condition and impede present-day relationships: members of the other great religions are afraid of being taken over and conquered, of suffering a sort of cultural colonization. Inbuilt ways of living and regarding Christianity, and of considering other religions, make it difficult for existing Christian communities to make the change asked or required of them. On the other side, despite their tolerance, Asiatic religions are also convinced of their superiority over Christianity, and try to bring it into their own orbit by reinterpreting it in terms of their own traditions.

EVANGELIZATION IN THE OVERALL MISSION OF THE CHURCH

The term 'evangelization' can be understood in different ways. Here I intend it in the restricted sense of the process by which Christ is presented to those who have not yet chosen him (initial evangelization, evangelization for conversion), or the process by which Christ, once accepted, is confronted so as to become the centre of one's life, a process of renewal and progress, whether on a personal or community level (self-evangelization).

Taken in this sense, evangelization does not embrace the whole mission of the Church, particularly in this situation.[11] This should be the implanting of the love of the Trinity and Christ in determined cultures and particular societies. It is within this overall requirement of charity that the mission takes on its particular forms, dictated both by the quality of divine love incarnate in Christ and by the needs of the men to whom it is directed. Charity remains the ultimate criterion by which the forms it takes and its particular modes of application must be judged. If they are to realize this charity, the different forms of mission can be grouped in this triple common task:

1. To recognize the presence and activity of God in human society, collaborating with it in its advancement. Today this takes particular shape in efforts toward development and the inter-religious dialogue.[12] The Church has the duty to be a sign and sacrament of salvation to the whole of mankind: it should help Buddhism progress along its own course of the history of salvation, and in a way work to make the Buddhist a better Buddhist. In a word, the Church should, in a given situation, become the motive force of the saving work of God and of the human quest for integral liberation.

2. To live in and witness to Christ in a particular culture. This concerns evangelization both within and outside the community of believers. Evangelization is not only the preaching of Christ as an historical personage, but should also be the manifestation of the Christ who lives in the community of the faithful, and, finally, the revelation of the Christ present and active in the individuals and culture of the people to whom it is directed.[13] Hence the pastoral, as well as theological importance of a Church that is the sign of the witness of its members, as well as of its activities and structures. This work of evangelization is carried out through the lives of Christians, through their deeds as well as through their words, as the Synod, developing the reflections of the Council, has shown.[14]

I shall limit myself here to stressing two particular requirements. In the first place, the message must be presented to the followers of the Asiatic religious traditions in such a way that they can correctly grasp its meaning. In the second, Christian proselytes from these traditions must be presented with the message in a manner that is not only intelligible but also enlivening: their entry into and progress in the Christian life must not imply rejection or diminution of the authentic values they have formerly lived by—or should have lived by; their conversion to Christ should assure the safeguarding, deepening and enrichment of these same religious and cultural values.

3. To realize that incarnating Christ in a given culture does not mean merely founding a Church, but deepening the experience of Christ in a particular context, taking on its aspirations and values. This is a task that will not be fully accomplished till Christ comes in glory.

Evangelization has to take its place within this overall missionary endeavour. It is not enough to proclaim the message in a comprehensible and challenging way; the Church, in its universal and above all its local incarnation, must be made desirable and accessible to Asians; it must be faithful to and redolent of the Christ who constitutes its whole *raison d'être* and gives it its originality.[15] It must be seen to uphold the values considered essential in religious tradition, such as contemplation, and the aspirations and social needs of present-day society, such as desire for justice and for the renewal of society.[16]

Presentation of the Christian message to members of other Asian religions is bedevilled by a particular problem: that of language. The message is either incomprehensible to them, or they understand it in a defective form. Buddhists, for example, cannot find in it a joyous and liberating announcement of final salvation for mankind, nor of the means to achieve this. So the message does not come to them as a response to their inner purpose, to their ideals. Nor can they see in it an authentic spiritual orientation and teaching that bears some relation to, or better still, agrees in some way with, the spiritual teaching of their Master. From their point of view, this message does not deserve to be accepted either by those advanced in spirituality, who have already attained a higher degree, or by ordinary Buddhists, who have the equivalent in their own rites and teachings, and their own expectation of gaining the happiness of the heavens and the gods. So it must be said that the Good News of Christ has not yet been implanted in the minds or the hearts of Buddhists, or of followers of the other great religions, in such a way as to make them feel bound to opt of their own free will for Christ and his followers. The genuine conversion of some of them does not invalidate this general conclusion, since most of those who are converted in this way have already had some previous contact with Western culture and its religious ideals.

The criteria for a solution to this problem can be found in a double orientation: toward a deepening of understanding and experience of the Christian kerygma, and toward deeper understanding not only of Buddhists' categories and language, but of their spiritual quest, of their overall aim, their hope, their approach to salvation. The good news will become intelligible to the extent that it is expressed according to the thought-processes of those who receive it, so that they can grasp its meaning. The news is good when it responds to a deep longing, and, at the same time, when it appears capable of realization in itself, because it has already been realized, or is in process of being realized, in the lives of those who proclaim it. The news is acceptable when it respects and honours the currents of wisdom and spirituality of the traditions of those to whom it is addressed, and the achievements of those who represent and have embodied the greatest realizations of these values.

This reflection on how the message might be re-expressed for Buddhists has been dealt with in greater depth elsewhere,[17] with a development of the two criteria, and a sketch of the message represented, indicating stages, motives and unsolved questions. In the Buddhist situation one would, for example, start with man, with his knowledge of the evil that is in him and his quest for salvation, moving on to the call of Christ, who reveals the ultimate end, God the Father, and invites man to experience this definitive liberation with him.

Research into this re-expression should of course take account not only of the specificity and basic aim of each religion, but also of the different groups adhering to it, since these religions are movements with different degrees of belonging, with varied and graded visions and experiences, with tendencies that favour assimilations to and symbioses of differing traditions. A message adapted in this way can serve as a first proclamation and then for devising a new approach to catechesis in this situation.

This revision of language and its use should not be seen as a shortcut to conversions. Conversion depends on God's plan and work, and on man's response to it. The Church's task is not to count the number of conversions but to be the valid instrument of a faithful mission, one that always respects God's freedom of action and man's freedom of response.

THE POSSIBILITY OF CHRISTIAN BUDDHISM

The question of whether it is possible to be Buddhist and Christian at the same time is one that preoccupies not only Western and Eastern intellectuals, but also simple people in remote villages. This indicates a natural sympathy on their part toward Christianity, coupled with a fear that by adopting it they will be cut off from their own culture and people. Many societies show an identity between belonging to a culture and to the dominant religion: in Thailand the terms Thai and Buddhist are interchangeable; in Burma, Burmese and Buddhist; in Cambodia, Khmer and Buddhist, at least till the installation of the present regime. In some countries, not being Buddhist debars one from the centre of society, or at least from certain posts of responsibility. This socio-religious situation perhaps explains the decline in Christian numbers in countries like Sri-Lanka.

It is commonly claimed that the Church must become Japanese, Indian, Thai, and so on, while remaining Catholic—indeed, in order to remain Catholic, in order to be a comprehensible sign and an adequate vehicle for its mission. It is less usual to have the courage to express this in religious terms and say Buddhist-Christian or Hindu-Christian, simply because this juxtaposes two realities of the same order. Without going into the question of whether Christianity is a religion or only a faith, or whether Buddhism is a religion or only a way of spiritual experience, one can say that every religion has a physiognomy of its own, with a system of values, functions and models. One has to take account of the existential whole of a religious movement, not just one aspect of it.

Before approaching an answer to whether a Christian Buddhism is possible, let us look a little more closely at what is envisaged. We are dealing with situations and experiences that have not been closely examined, but rather willed to come about. Even when they try to avoid any 'contamination by other superstitious religions', many Buddhist converts to Christianity, or Christians who live in a Buddhist culture, have been influenced by Buddhism in their understanding and experience of Christianity. For example, the concept of merit is understood and practised in a Buddhist perspective; the same can be said of their view of sin, the religious life and the Church. This becomes clear from any serious dialogue that avoids stereotyped responses. There have been Christian groups who remained animist at the same time, practising the rites of the two traditions. But most Christian communities break with their previous religious models and practises. This break was easier in the past, when Christians often lived apart, in separate communities, either in remote rural areas or in urban ghettoes. The influences surrounding them affected their manner of understanding Christian worship, religious practices, Church structures, and so on.

These experiences show that syncretism is a religious disease ever lying in wait. It is impossible to avoid either the 'tabula rasa' approach common enough in the missionary methods of the past, or leaving two religious traditions to live together, following a Buddhist type of missionary practice. If there is to be a way out, it has to be through each individual and each community working for unity from the starting-point of their basic concepts, from the nucleus of their specific religious experience. For a Christian synthesis, Christ has to be discovered and accepted in a radical fashion, as the *crisis* of all things, as the paschal mystery, as the only saviour, even though he is also the culmination of every human-divine way. This centrality has to be retained, or rather continually renewed, especially at times of change and adjustment. This indicates the need for self-evangelization, and the difficulties in the way of a successful synthesis.

Certain individuals in different parts of Asia, and some Ashrams in India, have undertaken conscious research into this sort of synthesis, but their experience is still too recent for general conclusions to be drawn from it, though it has produced beneficial results that have spread to surrounding communities. There is certainly no escaping such a meeting and reciprocal influence of the two religions, because of the new social situation, in which Christians live immersed in the non-Christian mass, through the process of urbanization and the growth of all means of social communication. This immersion in present-day society presents new challenges to Christian witness and perseverance. Loss of traditionally-rooted faith is not only a problem in the West, but a universal one, characteristic of the processes of urbanization and migration.[18]

AN OUTLINE THEORETICAL ANSWER

It is not easy, either, to say whether it is possible to be a Christian Buddhist, or whether Christian Buddhism is possible, from the theoretical standpoint. One has to start by defining the elements that make up a Christian or a Buddhist, what is involved in Buddhism as a spiritual and social movement, and what elements are necessary to the community of the disciples of Christ. Then we must see if mutual coexistence is possible, at what levels, and on what conditions. Finally, we need to see if coexistence will be accepted by the religious-social bodies concerned in it. All this shows how complex the question is on the theoretical as well as the practical level, because it involves the specificity of each religion and its embodiment, personal authenticity and ecclesiology. A problem of this nature certainly cannot be taken lightly.

Both traditions, Buddhist and Christian, contain diverse elements and work on different levels, but both contain a kernel that conditions all the rest. For example, to judge from the totality of their tradition, the Buddhist masters distinguish three dimensions or levels: *dharma,* the central message of the Buddha, comprising the four fundamental truths and concomitant experience; *laddhi*, theoretical vision and religious beliefs, based on faith or the reasoning of a still worldly and immanentist nature; *paveni*, cultural and religious traditions, with their uses and customs, rites and practices. These three levels posit a hierarchy of truths: the first comes from the Buddha and constitutes the way of salvation, while the other two are external trappings and supports. Ordinary people and common practice, however, tend to combine them all in the same reality. Dialogue with the most open-minded and the evolving socio-religious mentality and situation can lead to an internal renewal of Buddhism and to Christian acculturation through this hierarchy of values. In the Christian sphere too, the earlier monolithic concept of truth is giving way to a hierarchization of values. The natural sciences have helped to a greater understanding of the relationship between theory and practice, between official and popular religion, between the teaching given and the meaning perceived. Modern ecclesiology is stressing the centrality of Christ and the hierarchy of all other elements.

By way of example, one can distinguish different levels in both traditions, which can be summarized thus:

—*Cultural*. Actions and behaviour that are cultural in origin, though influenced by religious outlook and experience, such as ways of organizing religious communities, ways of expressing veneration . . .
—*Ethical*. Moral actions, categories and values, which do not necessarily originate in the central message, though they are influenced by it.
—*Ritual*. The rites and ceremonies that accompany the religious expressions of the community and the individual.
—*Spiritual*. The preferred modes in which religious experience of the sacred and in particular of the Absolute are embodied: meditation, prayer, the religious life.
—*Fundamental*. Basic values that characterize each religion, such as Christian charity or Buddhist detachment.
—*Central*. The centre that qualifies and dynamizes all the rest: *dharma* for Buddhism and Christ in Christianity.[19] This basic concept hierarchizes everything and gives it meaning.

It is certainly possible to be both Buddhist and Christian on some levels, by adopting compatible elements. On the social and cultural levels this identity is necessary to be a fully integrated member of society. But even at these levels there are difficulties: the daily genuflection to the gods, for example, is a cultural act, but in the popular Buddhist view it is this that marks one as being a Buddhist and constitutes the layman's most important action. On the ethical level too, it is possible to achieve identity to a large extent: the categories and precepts of both religions are based on human experience. But one has to adopt values as well as categories, as is often demonstrated in the intervention of the hierarchy of values: the centrality of Christian charity affects not only motivations, but also decisions and the scale of values by which one judges one's actions.

On the ritual level, there is the triple problem of adapting Christian rites, adopting Buddhist rites and taking part in Buddhist worship. It is not only a question of finding a comprehensible symbolic framework, but also of adapting to the people's tempo and responding to their needs. Much can be done in this sphere.

On the level of spiritual experience, there are basic attitudes, ways of meditation and forms of religious life compatible with Christian understanding and experience. It is possible to imagine a community of Buddhist monks carrying on their traditional office and religious observances while at the same time leading a Christian life.

For some, this harmonization of elements on different levels could be seen as Christian Buddhism. But there are two difficulties in the way of this means of assimilation. In the first place, Buddhists could react against undue annexation by Christians. For example, when about twenty years ago a church was built in the style of a pagoda in Bangkok, the Buddhists attacked the concept, although there were already pagodas built in the style of churches. Then, the whole problem goes deeper than this. The adoption of certain behavioural models is not enough to change a whole basic approach; it gives rise to syncretism on the part of the individuals who adopt them, and gives a coat of varnish to the Church rather than an authentic embodiment.

On the Buddhist side, one can picture a community that strives to be Christian, while keeping its own traditions, adapting Christian principles and moral attitudes, beliefs and practices to suit them. On the individual level this is perhaps what happens in Japan, where the number of those who call themselves Christians is much greater than the number of members of the different Churches. Admitting the first hypothesis and the second interpretation, there still remains the problem of whether it is possible to be a Christian without belonging in any way to a community of disciples. But, in any case, a convergence of the two traditions would have to take place on a deeper level.

It would be possible to speak of a Christian Buddhism if one could put together a vital synthesis of the basic outlooks of the two traditions, if it was possible to weld the centres and the essential elements of the two ways together into a new whole, from which a unity of system and

a hierarchy of elements could derive. In short, the specificity and originality of the two experiences would have to be fused. And this, for both
psychological and theological reasons, seems to me impossible. Even
admitting that Buddhism is one way of salvation in God's plan, it is still
in a similar stage of development to Hebraism in relation to Christianity. It cannot be called Christianity unless Christ is its life-centre,
the principle of its judgments and choices, the underlying reason for its
unity and its hierarchization of elements. Take for example the Buddhist quest for and experience of the Absolute: this is felt as an existential choice of that which transcends all and as experience of the utterly
other, to which there can be no personal relationship, and of which one
can know nothing until joined to it. This attitude could help Christian
experience, but this would have to change both its content and its form,
because of the Christian concept of interpersonal relationship with God
the Father. It seems to me, therefore, that there can be no identification
on the deepest level. In the same way, the originality of Christianity
would change the spirit of the other levels of possible communion and
assimilation.

So this hypothetical Christian Buddhism, if it were to be centred on
the experience of Christ, would be a completely new Christian reality
in the encounter with Buddhism, even though it took some of its models, functions and values from it, and even if it took on its basic purpose
of perfect liberation. In order to become Christian, Buddhism would
have to undergo a paschal mystery, a process of death and resurrection, of loosing and re-binding. It would be a different vital synthesis,
which no methodology could create and no theology could describe in
advance. A Christian Buddhism is only possible in this sense and on
these conditions, at least in its final phase. This, of course, should not
exclude cross-fertilization and mutual influence of the two religions,
thanks to growing relationships of dialogue between them. But in this
case, each religion is keeping, deepening and purifying its own identity
and originality, and therefore its autonomy.

WORKING PRINCIPLES

The Churches of Asia, as elsewhere, must become embodied in, take
on the religious values of, and re-express their experience in a manner
meaningful to and therefore in relationship with the religion and culture
in which they exist. So in some way the Church in Thailand must
become Thai and Buddhist, along the lines indicated. There are some
working principles that can be laid down in order to bring this about.

The community of believers must make a constant effort at self-
conversion to Christ and incarnation in the society in which it finds
itself, taking on its present aspirations and purposes, not just its cul-

tural and religious traditions from the past. Acculturation means adopting what is living, and avoiding any adoption of what is in decline, even if Christianity has a duty to save some values that would otherwise be lost. It must constantly watch the hierarchy of Christian values, placing Christ always in the centre and adopting charity as the constant criterion of action. Self-evangelization—the meeting with Christ and his message—is the first criterion of and the first means to authentic acculturation.

One can make a distinction between already-formed Christian communities, with more or less adapted traditions, and communities of neophytes coming from religious backgrounds of this type. This second situation allows more scope for creativity. The emergence of groups of this kind will allow for acculturation in the local Churches and can play a dominant rôle. Without group conversions, it is difficult, not to say almost impossible, for a local Church to have vitality and become incarnate in the local culture.

In these new communities, the break with the past should not be premature or based on criteria of secondary importance. It must spring from personal and community conversion to Christ, or it will merely pass from one ritualism to another, one moralism to another. It must therefore be possible for a gradual path to be found, for the individual and the community, in a broader sense than was conceived and practised at the time of the catechumenate. The local Church will become a movement, with groups going forward at different speeds, but always in quest of a living Christ seeking to become incarnate there.

The understanding of the community, based on the constant challenge of Christ and a continual effort of charity, will be the basic guide to progress along these lines. The decisions of authority and the solutions of specialists can only be complementary to this process of incarnation. Communion with other believing communities and other local Churches should become ever closer, in order to prove and complete the community's own fidelity to Christ, and to communicate it to others.[20]

This stress on constant reference to Christ should not be taken as implying concentration on the Church to the exclusion of the world around it. Christ is certainly present in the Church, which he constantly challenges to better things, but he is also present in the world, building his Kingdom of love and justice. So the community must be humbly open to and in continual dialogue with its surrounding culture, in all its dimensions and its religious ones in particular, so as to understand it and serve it, and also so as to hear the call of God in it, to meet Christ in it and serve him, and so remain in a state of self-evangelization.

Translated by Paul Burns

Notes

1. FABC Secretariat, ed., *His Gospel to Our Peoples. Evangelization in the World Today* (Manila, 1976), 3 vols. Reviewed in M. Zago, 'Assemblée plenière des Conférences épiscopales d'Asie', in *Kerygma* 22 (1974), pp. 87-96; id., "Chiave di lettura", in *Semi del Vangelo* (Bologna, 1975), pp. 221-53; id., 'Evangelizzare oggi in Asia (Dialogo con le religione non cristiane)', in *Evangelizzare oggi* (Bologna, 1976), pp. 39-66.

2. M. Zago, Rites et cérémonies en milieu bouddhiste lao (Rome, 1972).

3. Idem, 'La conversion en milieu bouddhiste', in *Chemins de la conversion* (Paris, 1975), pp. 54-77.

4. F. Margiotti, 'La questione dei riti ciensi: Tentativi di adattamento', in *Evangelizzazione e Culture* II (Rome, 1976), pp. 269-96.

5. This view was expressed by Mgr. Kuo of China in the Fourth Congregation of the Fourth Synod; by Card. Parecattil of India in the Third Cong.; by Mgr. Kitbunchu of Thailand in the seventh.

6. A new theology of non-Christian religions was not only discussed but sketched out by the bishops of Asia in the Fourth Synod. Cf., for example, the declaration by the bishops of Taipei, and the interventions of Fernades (seventh), Kuo (tenth), Hadisumarta (twelfth), Gaviola (fourteenth) Picachy (fourth), and so on.

7. Cf. intervention of Mgr. Padiyara of India (Tenth Cong.) in which he quoted Gandhi: 'I love Christ, but not Christians, because Christians are not like Christ'.

8. Endo Shusako, in his novel *Silence* (Tokyo, 1972), puts this saying into the mouth of a Samurai: 'In one plot a tree grows, in another it withers. The tree of the Christian religion puts out leaves, buds and flowers in other countries, but in ours the leaves wither and there is not a bud to be seen. Different land, different water'. And the ex-Father Ferreira repeats this: 'This land is a fearful desert, more terrible than you can imagine. Anything planted immediately withers, the leaves turn yellow and fall; and we have planted the Christian religion right in the middle of this desert'.

9. The Catholic Church's teaching and charitable organizations often evoke the admiration of non-Christians in Asia. At least one group would like to involve the Church more closely in the work of development but in a less institutionalized form.

10. M. Zago, 'L'équivalent de "Dieu" dans le bouddhisme', in *Eglise et Théologie* 6 (1975), pp. 25-49, 153-74, 297-317.

11. Id., 'Missionary Pastoral Practice in a Laotian Buddhist Milieu', in *Teaching all Nations* IX (1972), pp. 287-304.

12. Id., 'Présence du Christianisme en Orient et dialogue', in *Kerygma* 21 (1973), pp. 147-72.

13. Id., 'Le Kérygme dans la perspective de *Gaudium et Spes*', in *Kerygma* 4 (1970), pp. 3-15.

14. Id., 'Historique du Synode sur l'évangelisation et prospectives pour la mission', in *Kerygma* 23 (1974), pp. 97-144; id., '1974 Synod: some Missionary Perspectives', in *Omnis Terra* 69 (1975), pp. 277-89.

15. The priority given by the bishops of Asia today to the indigenization of

the Churches in Asia in order to evangelize the continent can be understood in this perspective.

16. M. Zago, 'L'Evangile au Laos, force de libération?', in *Mission de l'Eglise* (Paris, 1974), pp. 3-11.

17. Id., 'Le message chrétien en milieu bouddhiste', *Lumen Vitae* XXIX (Brussels, 1974), pp. 77-107.

18. Id., 'L'indifferenza religiosa nel buddismo contemporaneo', in Miano, ed., *L'indifferenza religiosa* (Rome, 1977).

19. In Buddhism, what corresponds to Christ as centre of life and doctrine is *dharma*, that is the doctrine, truth, final law and liberation, which the Buddha, like so many others, discovered and embodied, teaching it to the men of his day. Buddha only shows the way, without being himself either way, or centre, or salvation.

20. M. Zago, 'Universal Church and Local Churches. Respective Tasks in the Encounter of the Gospel with Cultures', in *Omnis Terra* 82 (Rome, 1977), pp. 192-208.

Fernando Castillo

Evangelization in Latin America

DURING the last two decades there have been profound changes in the Church in Latin America. One sign of this renewal process is that 'evangelization' has increasingly become a central concern both in theory and the search for new practice in the Church.

The object of this paper is to point out some basic aspects of the problem of evangelization in Latin America. Briefly, it could be said that it is a problem of the relationship and tensions between past and future in the Latin American Church, between the affirmation of a Christian tradition rooted deep in Latin American societies and the radical criticism of these societies and the Church's rôle in them, between the empirical awareness of the 'Christian people' and Christian faith as the *praxis* of liberation and critical consciousness of society.

EVANGELIZATION IN A CHRISTIAN CONTINENT?

It may sound paradoxical to speak of evangelization in Latin America which is traditionally considered to be a Christian country. One of the characteristics of Spanish and Portuguese colonization was its cultural and religious aggressiveness. The process of colonization and Christianization went hand-in-hand. The colonizers rapidly imposed Christianity on the different cultures they found in Latin America, without taking into consideration the different levels of development they had reached. Of course there were important exceptions when bishops and missionaries who had come to the new lands defended the Indians against the ever-growing violence and exploitation of the colonizers. But taken as a whole the process of colonization involved the Church as a cultural domination apparatus, through which the structures of the indigenous cultures were destroyed—although not of course all their elements—and new cultural forms imposed. From this process there emerged on the one hand a popular Christianity (and popular cultures) which incorporated and fused many indigenous cultural elements into Christian beliefs and rites, and on the other hand, a Church which was solidly integrated into the structures of domination of the oligarchical colonial societies. In general, the criticism of popular Latin American piety has concentrated on the syncretism in the survival of magical indigenous elements as a degeneration of Christianity, while disregarding its exact counterpart, viz., the practical syncretism represented by the integration of the Church within the oligarchical structures of domination.

If we are going to take the problem of evangelization seriously, we must question the 'Christianity' which has crystallized in the oligarchical societies. This does not imply the rejection of popular piety as pure superstition or dismissing the Church as nothing but a mechanism of domination of the oppressed. The questions we must ask for the sake of evangelization mean, of course, breaking away from the mere repetition of past schemata, but it does not mean ignoring the historical and religious reality of Latin America. Popular Christianity and the Church are not mere statistical data, but historico-cultural dimensions with deep roots in the continent. With all their ambivalence, they are—like it or not—the Christianity which has existed and still does to a large extent in Latin America.

The context of our questioning is a social and historical crisis of vast proportions: the gradual awakening of the Latin American people, the marginal masses, their slow coming to consciousness and fighting for their freedom. This has caused a sharpening of social contradictions. Finally the crisis has come for the oligarchical society and its structures of domination. The storm has been gathering since the second decade of this century and broken in the last twenty years. After the weakening and discrediting of the old traditional oligarchies, and as a consequence of economic underdevelopment and dependence, the new industrial ruling classes did not succeed in attaining a hold sufficient to enable them to dominate completely. The marginalized popular masses increasingly pressed for a greater economic, political and cultural share in social life, and to create at last a new egalitarian society in which the people could be the subjects or enactors of their own history. It was this context of social crisis and conflict that saw the awakening, first, of small Christian groups and later of ever-growing sectors of the Church. A new awareness had arisen seeking, tentatively at first then persistently, to identify Christians and the Church as a religious and cultural dimension, with marginalized and oppressed people. The Church was growing conscious of the profound divisions and conflicts in Latin

American societies. The ruling classes responded to the threat to their power by increasing violence. The process of social change and democratization was drastically held back. A new type of military dictatorship took over in most Latin American countries to enable the ruling classes to keep their power .and privileges. Repression of popular movements reached tragic proportions.

In this situation the Church is confronted with a straight choice between being the Church of the powerful and the oppressors or the Church of the oppressed people. The choice it makes between these two alternatives will be decisive for its historical significance in Latin America as well as more particularly for the problem of evangelization. The development of the Church in recent years, its new awareness and new practices, allow us to hope that it is coming down more and more decidedly and firmly on the side of the poor and the oppressed. Of course there are exceptions and hesitations; often these represent attempts by Churches in rich countries to control and colonize Latin American Christianity once again.[1]

THE POOR HAVE THE GOSPEL PREACHED TO THEM

The Church's choice also determines the broad lines evangelization must take. In the face of this new historical challenge, the Church, by opting for the poor and oppressed, is more true to its origins. The Gospel becomes again a message preached firstly to the poor, to those that have neither money, power, nor status.

Choosing the poor does not involve a romantic attitude which glorifies the virtues of poverty. This would be a terrible mistake in the Latin American situation. The poverty in which great numbers of Latin Americans live and suffer means sub-human living conditions, insecurity, daily grinding humiliation, and a life of obscurity offering no way out. Neither does this choice mean choosing poverty as an abstract life ideal, but an involvement with the poor as a burning reality, which urges and challenges the Christian conscience.

This means that the evangelization of the poor must take place from within their world. For centuries the Church and its preaching have been present among the poor, but because of the Church's position in the social structure, it came as something from outside and fundamentally alien to them. But now evangelization must mean a new presence of the Church among the oppressed, that is to say, a real coming to them so that it really is the people's Church. Real solidarity with the oppressed is a condition for evangelization. It has been fulfilled by Christians who have taken the decision to live like the people and share their poverty and sufferings.[2] A Latin American bishop expressed it thus directly: 'I want to urge you that we should avoid the danger of becoming so used to the poverty we see in the streets that we walk by on the other side or avoid it with blindfolded eyes. The Church, like Jesus on the road to Emmaus, will only be recognized by its fraternal sharing. This is the condition for its credibility. Now evangelization must have a visible face which is called solidarity.'[3] This means that in Latin America especially, evangelization cannot be understood as mere word, valid just for itself. First and foremost it must be action, as the practice of Christians, one of whose tools is the Word.

The Gospel preached to the oppressed is not a word of resignation or consolation, but news that in spite of the weight of injustice and oppression under which they suffer now, they are called to be free to the full, and human to the full: in spite of their daily misery, hunger, lack of 'education', in spite of the apparent omnipotence of the ruling classes and the military dictatorships with their apparatuses of terror. The message is that this vocation to freedom cannot be renounced, that nothing and no one has the right to cancel it, that the call to freedom comes from Jesus himself, the Son of God, who was also poor and persecuted by the powerful, and who ratified and sealed definitively the call to freedom with his own suffering. The solidarity of Christians and the Church with the oppressed should try to be a sign and a proclamation of Christ's own solidarity with them: a sign of suffering solidarity which is also freedom-seeking.

Thus evangelization operates as a 'subversive' factor in the social reality of Latin America dominated by injustice and the violence of the powerful. The proclamation of freedom cannot help but become a markedly political message. If it did not, the preaching of the Gospel would be a vague platitude which would totally discredit Christ's solidarity with the oppressed. What possible meaning could it have for an exploited worker or a man out of work to be preached a freedom which said nothing about the urgent problems they were facing, of being laid off, of union rights and liberties, the need to change the system of exploitation? What would freedom mean to the peasant if it said nothing about the land problem, the *latifundio* and the need for agrarian reform? What would a message of freedom mean for the oppressed in Latin America if it did not attack head-on and actively the *régimes* of terror that the ruling classes have imposed on the people? If evangelization is to be based on solidarity with the oppressed, this means that it cannot ignore the close connection between the freedom promised in Christ and the political and social freedom desired and sought after by the people. God's freedom and love proclaimed in the Gospel would be an empty formula if they did not take on the human and political aspirations of the poor and their struggle for liberation.[4]

Finally, the political dimension of evangelization implies the realization that the poor and the oppressed, to whom the Gospel is preached, are not individuals or an isolated phenomenon, but that they have a social and economic identity and are of great structural importance in Latin American societies. They are particular social classes, which the system of domination has marginalized from political and cultural life and whose share in the economy has reduced them to being objects of exploitation by capital. This makes it even clearer that the evangelization of the poor requires that the Church should 'change places' in the social structure. It must not only take on the material living conditions of these classes, but take sides with them and join in their political aspirations. Thus the Church will acquire a new identity, as a symbol of the people's hopes for liberation.

EVANGELIZATION AND POPULAR RELIGION

When the Church turns to the people, popular religion then becomes a particularly important problem for evangelization. As we mentioned earlier, popular Latin American Christianity was a product of the process of colonization and the Church's part in it, and of the fragments of indigenous cultures which managed to survive and become incorporated into the new religion. The result was a rural religion corresponding to the agrarian societies which had formed in Latin America. It is impossible to sum up this religion in brief. Certain saints and the Virgin Mary have a primary rôle in it and popular devotions revolve round them; it is far from being a Christo-centric religion. The special saints were those linked by Catholic devotion to the life cycle or the fertility cycle of the earth (those who helped you to get a husband, have a child, cure certain illnesses, get good harvests, rain, and so on). This kind of religion had a stabilizing function in the social system. However we should not forget that this was possible precisely because it captured protest impulses against the existing social order within particular religious symbols and annulled and redirected them in order to consolidate that order. Thus it contributed politically to a static view of the world and society and to sacralizing the *status quo*.

There is no doubt that the crisis in agrarian society has also meant a crisis in popular religion, but we should also realize that there is no direct or mechanical correspondence between the level of socio-economic structures and culture. Popular religion is far from being a phenomenon of the past, it is still going strong, to a greater or lesser extent, as the religion of the masses. Various sectors of the Church have tried to cope with this problem by different attitudes and pastoral alternatives.[5] Between the extremes of a conservative line which would allow popular piety to carry on uncriticized, and a 'liberal' élitist line which rejects popular religion as pagan superstition and ignores its historical roots among the people, there is an attempt to preach the Gospel which accepts the people as they really are but at the same time urges them to struggle for liberation. Accepting the people as they really are means that evangelization cannot ignore the great religious and cultural strength of popular religion: that is to say, the Gospel is being preached to people whose historical culture traditionally regards Christianity as, if not openly against liberation, at least highly ambiguous towards it. But we should also realize that these are the symbols that have been nursed by the religious experience of the people, and that their experience of suffering and search for liberation are also involved in them. Evangelization which is genuinely directed towards the people must be fully aware of the ambiguity in popular religion. Hence various theological attempts are being made to show the need for evangelizing popular Christianity and to preach the Gospel in a way that will raise the consciousness of the people.[6] This preaching would critically accept elements of popular religion and try to unearth the impulses towards Christian liberation which are buried in them.

Translated by Dinah Livingstone

Notes

1. A notorious example of these attempts is the campaign of theological repression against the theology of Latin American liberation organized in the Federal Republic of Germany by the leaders of Adveniat.

2. In this context poverty acquires its dimension as a symbol of solidarity with the poor and also as a protest against their enforced poverty. Cf. G. Gutierrez, *Evangelio y praxis de liberacion: Fe cristiana y cambio social en America Latina* (Salamanca, 1973), p. 238. See also, id., *Theology of Liberation* (Maryknoll, 1974).

3. Mons. F. Ariztia, *Algunas reflexiones sobre la solidaridad,* Christmas message (Santiago, 1974).

4. The emphasis on the link between political involvement in liberation and Christian faith is the central point of the Latin American 'theology of liberation'. Cf. Gutierrez, *Theology of Liberation.*

5. Cf. S. Galilea, *La fe como principio critico de promocion de la religiosidad popular: Fe cristiana y cambio social en America Latina* (Salamanca, 1973), pp. 156-58.

6. Cf. Gutierrez, *Theology of Liberation.*

Tamás Nyíri

Evangelization in the Socialist States of Eastern Europe

THE BACKGROUND TO THE QUESTION

Its justification

WE MUST first deal with possible misunderstandings. While the situation of the Church in the Socialist states shows common features, there are also significant differences. As a Hungarian theologian, therefore, I can write with a degree of competence only about my own country. On the other hand it might be asked whether evangelization in the industrialized areas of Europe faces the same problems as in socialist Hungary, a country with a Christian tradition of over a thousand years.

The Roman Catholic Church in Hungary has eleven dioceses, including three archdioceses and one joint Greek-Catholic diocese. Theological education takes place in five diocesan seminaries and the Theological Academy of Budapest, as well as at the Hungarian Pontifical Institute in Rome.

Since there are no official Hungarian statistics of church membership, calculations are based on family membership. On this basis it is estimated that, out of a population of 10.5 million, there are seven million Catholics, one and a half million Reformed Christians and 400,000 Lutherans. The number of convinced atheists is probably between 500,000 and 600,000. 46.0% of the population classify themselves as 'religious': 58.8% of agricultural workers, 47.3% of industrial workers, 31.2% of skilled workers and around 21% of intellectuals.[1]

Nevertheless resources for evangelization are modest. There is a good and independent, but relatively small, Catholic press. Books can be published, there are Church radio broadcasts, and there are eight Catholic high schools. The Theological Academy is open to laypeople.

Mention should also be made of the internal resources for the propagation of the faith, priestly work with individuals, preaching, catechesis and the optional religious instruction in schools and churches.

The historical background

The present situation has historical roots. Until 1945 the Hungarian Church had been able to retain all its medieval privileges and its secular power. The revolutionary transformation of Hungarian society and the separation between Church and State led to the total loss of these. Against this background and in view of the Marxist theory of religion, it is not surprising that religion and the Church were subjected to a fundamental challenge, and their days were regarded as numbered. At first the Church turned to political opposition, in which it was supported by the Vatican. This attitude, and the counter-measures it provoked, brought the Church to the verge of ruin. In this long internal and external battle, it was not preserved from wrong decisions and mistaken repression. Finally the Hungarian Church recognized Socialism (as a social system) and the Marxist state as realities. At the same time it came to be realized that the task given to the Hungarian Church by the Lord of history is to preach the Gospel in this place and under these conditions.

The turning-point in this process was the partial agreement between the Vatican and the Hungarian government in 1964. With the naming of L. Lékai as Archbishop of Esztergom and Primate of Hungary, all the sees were once more filled with resident bishops in 1976. In June 1977 Paul VI received Janos Kadar, the first secretary of the party, in private audience. At the end of the conversation, which lasted an hour, the Pope described this visit as the end of a slow but never interrupted process. The Pope said that the aim of the dialogue between the Vatican and the Hungarian state had been to secure the unity and loyal co-operation of all sectors of the population for the benefit of the whole nation in a climate of genuine religious peace. Hungary's Church and the Vatican were ready to continue on the path of positive co-operation. Mr. Kadar expressed similar views and paid tribute to the moral force and ethical value of the Church.

The present situation

None of this implies, however, that the situation of the Church is satisfactory. The situation was discussed by Cardinal Lékai after his appointment as Archbishop of Esztergom in an interview with the Hungarian news agency MTI. The cardinal mentioned four main prob-

lems: (1) the need for a satisfactory arrangement for religious instruction in the churches; (2) the need to involve a greater number of
laypeople in the official life of the Church and in evangelization; (3) an
up-to-date organization of the Church's pastoral work, with special
regard to ensuring a new generation of priests in view of the aging of
the clergy, resignations and the small number of seminarians (by 1990
the number of active priests is expected to fall by a half); [2] (4) the most
important task of making good the lack of information about the state
of the Church in Hungary.

Understanding the concept of evangelization

If the meaning of the concept of 'evangelization' is not sufficiently
clarified, its vagueness becomes particularly obvious in the conditions
of evangelization in a Socialist country. In Hungary orthodox teaching
had been presented to the faithful for centuries in the form of preaching
which originated at the Counter-Reformation. When the Church lost its
privileges, the blind alley into which this view of preaching had led the
Church became clear. Less than half the faithful had been able to
develop a mature personal faith. This showed clearly that the restric-
tion of evangelization to verbal preaching and rational argument as
practised by the specialists was not capable of providing foundations
for faith, let alone transmitting the good news.

One effect of these factors is that the level of religious interest among
intellectuals is markedly lower (21%) than in the other sectors of the
population. Anti-religious prejudices are particularly strongly marked
among the educated, and this situation is made worse by the lack of
education among priests, who feel helpless in the face of modern anti-
religious theories. All this indicates that as the general level of education rises evangelization in the sense of the purely verbal imparting of a
doctrine is less and less adequate to its task. It is therefore all the more
necessary to find new approaches.

Breaking down barriers

Before the new approaches can work, there are obstacles to be removed. The traditional patterns of speech used in preaching (a typical insiders' language and dysfunctional clichés are still common) are inadequate for arousing interest and communicating the essential message in a suitable way (*sufficiens praedicatio*). This sort of religious language, a clinging to outdated habits of thought, and the Church's self-image inevitably damage from the start the chances of any evangelization, the processes of communication which can establish faith and deepen it where it already exists.[3]

It is not surprising that feelings of hostility to the Church should appear particularly in countries with a long tradition of Christianity. In the minds of the more educated this is accompanied by a suspicion of religion as an ideology. In these circumstances it is understandable that believers in a Socialist country may be unable to deal by argument with the objections to which they are daily exposed, particularly when the clergy are unable to give satisfactory answers to particular problems faced by Christians in the modern world.

Personal witness in a living community

'Faith comes from what is heard' (Rom 10:17). While this statement is of fundamental importance for the basic structure of evangelization, there are plenty of other scriptural texts which stress 'lived witness' (Mt 5:13-6; 1 Pet 2:12, etc.). The preaching of the word and personal witness is always supported by the disciples' community of brotherly love (Acts 2:44-7; 4:32-3; 5:12-4). After the failure of the Jewish mission, the young Church abandoned any explicitly missionary activity and left evangelization completely to God (Acts 2:47), and still people joined the Church in increasing numbers. According to Pliny the Younger, Christianity spread in Bithynia like an epidemic.[4] The image of infection implies that the Christians increased, not as a result of propaganda, but organically, through their mere existence. The most important factor was personal contact,[5] in which everything depended on the quality of the Christian life of the communities. Even Justin does not attribute his conversion to philosophy: 'For at that time they did not first look for proofs to present their teachings; they do without proof completely, and yet are credible witnesses to the truth.' In the Christian community Justin encountered the spirit of God: 'Immediately my soul began to burn and I was seized with love for the prophets and the men who are the friends of Christ.'[6] However, even a rigorist like Tertullian invokes the help of the philosophy he claims to reject as soon as he has to produce a convincing theology. And it would indeed be senseless to reject the help of philosophy completely. This was accepted by the second century.[7]

In the face of the increasing de-Christianization of all industrialized countries, there can be little doubt that the existing form of evangelization is inadequate. As long as religious language is not reinforced by the experience that Christ lives on in his community, preaching does not go beyond words. Strong community life thus turns out to be one of the most important prerequisites of evangelization. This applies particularly to those countries in which the Church has been relieved of the 'burden' of its earthly power and also given a smaller scope for its activities. The collapse of a sort of state Church is itself an incentive to follow an approach to evangelization which corresponds best to the central aims of the task, namely the formation of Church communities.

The formation of Church communities and groups

Even today in Hungary, God rouses people to living faith, though they have not been called by anyone. There are men and women of prayer, 'baptized' by God himself with spirit and fire. There are men and women filled with love, and willing to take up the cross. Little communities of this sort, linked to their parish and the Church, form the vital centre of evangelization.

There have been small groups in the Church in Hungary since the end of the second world war, and in recent years they have probably grown in number and importance. 'We realize,' said Cardinal Lékai in an interview with Vatican Radio, 'that many of our faithful, men and women, are filled with a deep longing for a richer spirituality, and we are anxious to find a way of satisfying their wish.' There are increasing signs that the existence and activity of small groups within the Church are being permitted within clearly defined limits. 'All solid techniques of modern pastoral care can and must be used in pastoral work in Hungary.'[8] This applies particularly to learning processes in the faith which reflect the laws of social communication and modern learning theory. Equally a parish only grows into a genuine community in faith through the formation of living groups.[9]

On the other hand, the groups which spring up on the fringe of the Church's official structures can neither take over the full range of functions of Church life nor contribute to evangelization in the parish. This makes it quite understandable that the official Church authorities should regard small groups as a problem, an attitude reinforced by the state authorities' unhappiness with such fringe groups.

Awareness of the need for small groups as an integral part of the Church is still far from universal. For far too long the Hungarian clergy have spent their time bemoaning the past and closing their eyes to the real pastoral situation by stressing the 'full churches'. Elaborate Church plant and institutions in general have nothing like the importance once attributed to them.

Currently in Hungary 60.5% of all children born are baptized in Catholic churches; 60.9% of funerals and 37.3% of marriages are Catholic.[10] These figures show that there still remain great opportunities for evangelization in the form described above. It takes place in the existing parishes, but it only performs its task properly when it is carried out by groups in which the Spirit of God can be felt at work in the faith and love of the community. Such groups have great impact, and their existence and loyalty is an answer both to the anti-religious arguments of the Marxists and to the slight unease felt by the authorities of State and Church.

Translated by Francis McDonagh

Notes

1. T. Nyíri, 'Világi keresztények', : *Vigilia* 41 (1976), pp. 303-11, quotation from 303.

2. According to official statistics, resignations from the priesthood in Hungary are proportionately the highest in Europe. They are exceeded only by those of Brazil. Cf. E. Colagiovanni, *Crisi vere e false del prete* (Rome, 1973); T. Nyíri, 'Come vive il clero magiaro': *CSEO documentazione* 7 (1973), pp. 91-98; ibid., 'Godsdienstigheid en ateisme en Hongarije; enkele aspecten': *Wending* 32 (1977), pp. 39-50.

3. Cf. E. Bartsch and others, *Verkündigung. Pastorale. Handreichungen für den pastoralen Dienst* (Mainz, 1970), p. 9.

4. Ep. X, 96.

5. Origen, *Contra Celsum* III, 50 (*Sour. chrét.*, 136, pp. 118-20).

6. *Dial. cum Tryphone Jud.*, VII, 2; VIII, 1 (PG 6:492), translated from the German.

7. One need only mention Justin, Quadratus, Tatian and Cyprian.

8. A. Szennay & F. Tomka, 'Egyházi kisközösségek': *Teológia* 11 (1977), pp. 118-23, quotation from 121. The author is indebted to F. Tomka for other valuable suggestions for the article.

9. Cf. J. Müller, 'Gemeinde als Lerngemeinschaft', H. Erharter et al., *Prophetische Diakonie* (Vienna, 1977), pp. 139-46.

10. B. Csanád, 'A katolikus vallásosság mérése hazánkban': *Vigilia* 41 (1976), pp. 294-303, quotation from 299.

Pierre Talec

Evangelization and Christendom in the Countries of the West

CHRISTENDOM, evangelization: the two words together acquire a provoking ring. While this binomial could have made up a couple whose union gave birth to a flourishing Christianity, the fact is that so many centuries of Christian religion in the western regions of Christendom have produced a miscarriage. Many would in fact say that this Christendom has failed to give birth to an authentically evangelical Christianity. Jean Delumeau of the *College de France*, in his work *Le Christianisme va-t-il mourir?*, has no hesitation in stating that Christendom is a myth. A delusion. Not, admittedly, in the cultural sense of the word, since Christendom undeniably embraces centuries of Christian civilization, but in the radical meaning of the word 'evangelize', in which sense one can claim that it has not been evangelized. It has not produced a complete change of heart, has not converted the world.

In short, faced with this fiasco and the growing progress of atheism, Marxist criticism of religion as alienating and the disillusionment with Christianity felt by Christians themselves, there is clearly no point in asking whether the aim of evangelization should be to build a Christendom, but merely how to get out of the mess we are in!

Can one go back to the beginning? An impossible temptation and a senseless question, because even if the weight of the centuries provides a certain handicap, it also constitutes an undeniable wealth: the imperishable treasure of Tradition is welded to this historical matrix. Furthermore, we cannot command the collective memory of a race: it is not for us to try to efface the traces of a Christendom anchored in the depths of people's mentality. So, faced with the landslip representing the switch from Christianity to 'Christendom', how do we set about the task of evangelizing today?

AN HISTORICAL APPROACH TO THE QUESTION

First observation: the Christendom-Church block

There is now a block between Christendom and the Church. Naturally enough, a classic process of transference has led to the Church being saddled with the complaints that should be addressed to the Christendom of former days. This fatal term 'Christendom' has become so synonymous with collusion between Church and Power that there is now a spontaneous quest for a way to disentangle the Church from the world in order to regain a healthy approach to evangelization. So some people are asking: 'Is it enough for an ecclesial life centred on itself to exist in the West, or must our surroundings, largely alien to the Church, be changed in some way or other?'. Since these alien surroundings are undoubtedly the world, let us try to find what lies behind a question that seems to oppose the world to the Church.

Second observation: a dualist problem

Since the heyday of Christendom when Church and world were happily married, their relationship has deteriorated. The world became suspicious of the Church, and *vice versa*. Then the Second Vatican Council made a real effort to stop sulking at the world, and the conciliar period was full of talk of 'the open Church', the 'Church present to the world', and so on. We are far from a Church opposed to the world. But with the best of intentions, the Vatican II position is still a face-to-face one—gazing into each other's eyes, maybe, but still dualist. In the lands that knew 'Christendom', the current problem is how to work a cleavage that will finally allow the Church to be 'in the world' without being 'of the world'—avoiding the Constantinian confusion of 'the world with the Church' and without setting the two on parallel courses. The problem, in fact, of how to be the salt of the earth and the leaven in the dough. So the task for evangelization today, in land furrowed by Christian history, would seem to be how to find some ingenious way of making the seed and the soil one and the same. Once more, we are back with the problem of the relationship between the Church and the world.

In the broadest terms, and simplifying as much as possible, let us try to set out some historical markers:

(1) Constantinian era: *confusion* of Church and world;
(2) Era of progressive secularization: *opposition* between Church and world;
(3) Conciliar era, Vatican II: the Church wishing to be *present to* the world;
(4) Contemporary era: the Church *in* the world.

This scheme is not without its pitfalls, since it lands us in a situation where we risk repeating the misdeeds of the Constantinian confusion. If today's militants preach a certain separatism between the Church and the world, it is not for fear of seeing the Church brought down to the level of the world, as in the era of Christendom, but for fear of seeing the world reject the Church as being the chief obstacle to evangelization. It hardly needs repeating that the reproaches and criticisms still addressed to the Church are so wide-ranging that its institution can be considered a brake on the process of evangelization. So the Church in the world has to be understood as a Church not imposing itself in its triumphalist visibility but present in its vulnerability: 'For it is when I am weak that I am strong' (2 Cor 12:10). The Church must apply Paul's words to itself. It must be a retiring Church, drawn back from the shore like the sea at low tide, distant but present. This is a difficult balance to achieve, since if the Church withdraws too far into its shell it runs the risk of becoming invisible, of no longer making a sign, no longer being a sacrament.

A THEOLOGICAL APPROACH TO THE QUESTION

Word and ideology

The evangelization of the world is always the evangelization of the Church. Since Pentecost, the risen Christ has provided no revelation outside his body, the Church. So, whatever *impedimenta* the weight of the institution and its sins represent, to do without the Church is to betray evangelization. The call to faith that is the purpose of proclaiming the Word can only be a call to the faith of the Church. There is no faith in the risen Christ except an ecclesial faith. This amounts to saying that the structure of faith is sacramental. What does this mean? 'No one has seen God'. That is, no one has seen God directly. The Church is the *sign* that Jesus is the way. The Church is the *herald* of the Word, and it is in this sense that we can speak of the Church as sacrament; the Church is a mediation, not simply a means of access. To forget this structure of faith is to forget the sacramental structure of evangelization. In our old realms of Christendom, if we want not only to renew the sap in this concept of evangelization, but also to define its content, we have to uncover (or perhaps discover!) the fact that the Word of God is a sacrament in itself: it sends us back to ourselves and at the same time to what God wants to tell us today in and through the Church. I see this failure to recognize the sacramental dimension of the Word underlying the dualist Church-world opposition one comes up against in so many militant Christians. Our part of 'Christendom' cannot undig the ditch dug between sacrament and evangelization, a ditch that forces the observation that in the Church those who act are not the same as those who celebrate; there is a race of militants engaged in action and a (relative!) mass of practising Christians cut off from the world. This is serious. A word not relayed by action becomes a dead letter and a word not celebrated in faith becomes an ideology—and ideology makes the proclamation of the Gospel *a programme for society, not a proposition of faith*. It is the call to faith that justifies evangelization: not only announcing a Word new to its hearers, but interiorizing a Word provocative of conversion to the Spirit of the Gospel. This is a task that the residue of Christendom renders more difficult by overlaying the virulence of the call to *metanoia* with layers of old 'religion'.

An ecclesiology of the future: the Church-sacrament

The theology of Vatican II stressed the aspect of the Church as a sign to the nations. The French bishops, particularly Mgr. Coffy, were largely instrumental in the diffusion of this ecclesiology, which seems to avoid the dualist trap of opposing the world to the Church. Evangelization should not reckon on one or the other, but on both together. Declaring the Church-sacrament to be a sign of salvation in the world means that it is made of the same stuff as the world yet is somehow different. In the words of Mgr. Coffy: 'The Church is only sacrament to the extent that it is foreign, differentiates itself from the world so that questions can be asked'.

Cardinal Marty, Archbishop of Paris, gives an affirmative answer to the question of whether the Church in the West can live an ecclesial life centred on itself: 'Mission today refers us back to the fidelity of the Church, to its own identity, to the quality of the sign it gives'. One then has to ask how efficacious the quality of the sign is: how it is diffused and perceived? The sign 'Church' as such can only be effective when it meets its object: the world. This is why Cardinal Marty, careful not to see 'ecclesio-centrism' as a withdrawal, does not pose the false question of whether or not the Church should 'go out to the world'. 'It has no need to question itself on whether it should go out to the world; it is in the world. It bears the ordeals of all in itself'. So the Church-sacrament does not exist for itself; it is not the Church for the Church, nor the Church for the world, but the Church in the world as the salt of the earth. In this view of the Church-sacrament, the task of evangelization is to refer the world back to itself—a task that can clearly only be carried out in the world, since out of the ground the seed cannot survive. But equally, the task can only be carried out *by* the Church. Separating oneself from the Church the better to evangelize the world is to plunge back into a number of dead ends: Modernism (Immanentism), 'youth of the Church' (civilizing before evangelizing). One might add that wishing to cut oneself off from the Church in order better to evangelize the world means forgetting the collective dimension of evangelization. The evangelist today is not a Christian on his own, nor one of a small group of militants acting on their own account. Evangelists today are Christians dispersed in the world who meet to celebrate the mystery of their faith, and go out to live the Word in the field. But what field?

The Church: communion of churches

Many militants today are tired of choking down the institution so that the Church can present a more acceptable face to the world. Their efforts to make the Church more presentable are not to be despised, but this is not the way the world will be converted. To suppose that one day the Church's garment will be free from any stain or mark means that the adherence of faith will always be a free, purely gratuitous act. So they prefer to go down into the political marketplace where it is possible to change the world. It is not surprising that there should be a growing movement to relegate the Church to the sidelines, since in our piece of Christendom, it is not the Church that needs saving, but the world. The temptation to evangelize while leaving the Church out of account—without denying it, though—is explained by a tendency to regard the Church as still monolithically standing over against the world. We can go on saying, 'the Church is us', but in vain: the Church is still presented in terms of the archetype deeply engraved on the collective consciousness: 'Church-power', 'Church-institution', 'Church-hierarchy' . . . One remarkable fact is that those who reproach the Church for this monumental façade are always asking the official Church to pronounce on everything, as though the Church always had something to say about everything. In our world of outworn

Christendom, cannot the Church be guessed at as in early Christian times? Christians are not different from other men in the world, they are not separated from the world, but they are distinguished in order to 'make a sign' through their evangelical lives referred back to the risen Christ, in a communion of churches making up the One Church.

A PASTORAL APPROACH TO A FURTHERING OF THE QUESTION

Sacraments for all

The secularized terrain in which faith sprouts today is no longer spread out beneath us marked out like an airport. 'Little Christians' used to land on the strip of life 'well oiled' with the sacraments. These sacraments played the rôle of a driving belt producing more 'little Christians'. Not to mention the fact that the sacraments were also the channel for the transmission of political power in the Church. The ground of faith in the West today has suffered a certain amount of subsidence. Eroded by atheism, it provides rough going. This means that the whole world is no longer level. So who has to be evangelized? Unbelievers, certainly, but also those classes of Christians known, in Quebec for example, as 'distant', in France as *'mal croyants'*, 'sociological', 'seasonal', and so on. These Christians represent boggy but not impermeable ground, full of puddles, stones and tares— ambiguities providing obstacles to faith: religiosity, magical religion, fear of the next world, tainted motives, and so on. Working at grass-roots level on this soil that cannot be abandoned, more than one priest engaged in pastoral work at parish level has been able to claim that the sacraments provide a pastoral path to evangelization. The sacraments do indeed imply a basic evangelization that should already have been carried out. And it is often said that if evangelization is lacking, it cannot be made up for by the sacraments. Yet it must be said that a number of 'sociological Christians', asking to be married or for a child to be baptized, show a real willingness to receive the appropriate seed in their soil. So we must get away from an 'all or nothing' pastoral approach and recognize that requirements in the sacramental field cannot be levelled out. If it is to make a sign to Christians so diversified in their faith, the Church-sacrament has to develop a pastoral pluralism.

The needs of a pastoral pluralism

(1) To recognize different levels of faith

(2) To recognize different degrees of belonging to the Church
(3) To practise a demanding, not a lax, tolerance, measured by the
    breadth of the Spirit of Catholicity. So, for example, in a Christian
    family, baptism soon after birth remains highly desirable, but at the
    same time there should be a different form of baptism, a sort of
    acceptance into the Church, for parents who doubt or question.
    Engaged couples who do not feel able to commit themselves to
    living what the sacrament of marriage means in the Church, but
    who at the same time want some sign from God in their love, should
    not simply be shown the door. Perhaps we shall then accept that
    there is room for non-sacramental marriage in the Church? How-
    ever paradoxical it may seem, Christendom today is in a
    'cathechumenal' situation. We thought this was reserved to the
    'overseas' missions, but today it has become a pastoral norm in the
    de-Christianized countries of Christendom. So it is up to us to
    discover a new form of catechumenate that is not simply a direct
    preparation for baptism.

AN APPROACH TO UNBELIEF

The basic characteristic of the lands that made up Christendom is
today their atheism. But their atheism is not so simple, because it has
failed to uproot scraps of faith stuck in men's hearts like couch grass,
resisting the plough that turns the soil. Turning the soil to change men's
hearts—surely this is the starting-point for any evangelization? So
evangelization in the 'zones' of Christendom must surely be started by
living the Gospel as a force for health in the world? Voices other than
Christian ones are already making themselves heard. To pick one
among many, there is Herbert Marcuse—whom I cite not for the plea-
sure of adopting ideas from Marxist philosophers, but to remind us that
evangelization is not only a matter of bringing the good news in from
outside: we must also listen to the news brought from the world of
unbelievers. So Marcuse, with the concept of 'reification' explored in
One-dimensional Man, is on the side of Christians in that he reminds
them indirectly of the powerful challenge the Gospel can represent in
the world. The world thinks it can free itself from the slavery of
technological society by challenging the 'hyper-consumption' that
characterizes this society. But because the world fails to bring about a
radical break with the political and economic system that produced the
conditions for this society, because, in the final analysis, it has not been
converted, it 'leads its slavery back'. 'To be reified' is then conforming
to a subjecting cultural model, identifying oneself 'as subject' with the
stereotype of the object.

Faced with this phenomenon of reification, Christians in a society that has issued from Christendom need not only to act in order to evangelize, but to *re-act,* to act on the level of the *'res',* of the creature. They need to evangelize not with speeches and moralizing, but, 'freed from all ties', to evangelize through an art of living. This freedom to break from a gregarious world, one alienated by purchasing power, by the power drive, the sex drive, money, motor cars, holidays in the sun and social success, is a word indeed capable of turning the soil. So, is not the final aim of evangelization in our part of 'Christendom' to show that man, Christian man, is not one-dimensional, but that he has another dimension in God?

Translated by Paul Burns

Paul Löffler

The Ecumenical Problem in Evangelization

THE QUESTION

IN THEIR official statements, the Churches today speak with impressive unanimity about the *common* task of evangelization. Characteristic of such statements is the recurring appeal to Jn 17:21, with the explicit justification for unity 'so that the world may believe that thou hast sent me'. Statements of the World Council of Churches appeal to this justification, as did the Second Vatican Council's *Decree on Ecumenism,* which in its introduction described the sources of the effort for unity in these terms: 'Almost everyone, though in different ways, longs that there may be one visible Church of God, a Church truly universal and sent forth to the whole world that the world may be converted to the Gospel and so be saved, to the glory of God.'

The declaration by the fathers of the Synod at the end of the 1974 Episcopal Synod in Rome subsequently affirmed in much more specific terms its desire for collaboration in evangelization: 'In carrying out this task we wish to work in closer cooperation with Christians with whom we are not yet united in full 'Communio', and with their churches and ecclesial communities, on the basis of the one baptism and our common faith. In this we are led by the desire to present to the world, here and now, a broader common witness in evangelization for Christ'.[1]

It was clearly of symbolic significance that the General Secretary of the World Council of Churches was invited to Rome for this particular synod. In his address on 'Evangelization in the Modern World', Rev. P.A. Potter stressed in his turn the ecumenical significance of evangelization, which he called, in a phrase of Visser 't Hooft, 'the ecumenical theme *par excellence*'. 'It is part of this conviction that evangelization in the modern world can only be understood and carried out in an ecumenical perspective and in ecumenical cooperation.'[2] The Central Committee of the World Council of Churches, which dealt with the subject of evangelization once more at the beginning of August 1977, confirmed yet again the ecumenical commitment.

This recent ecclesiastical and theological discussion leads to the quite clear conclusion that there is a firm intention in principle to seek ecumenical co-operation in evangelization. The wish is clear, but the practical implementation lags far behind. A discussion of the ecumenical problems in evangelization must begin by explaining why this discrepancy exists.

DIFFICULTIES IN PRACTICAL ECCLESIOLOGY

Since the Second Vatican Council even ecclesiology has been cleared of several highly explosive problems for ecumenism. The Catholic Church has recognized the other churches in the major texts as legitimate churches or ecclesial communities in which salvation can be received. The underlying ecumenical theory is one of concentric circles, with, at the centre, the Catholic Church, alone endowed with the whole fulness of salvation. This necessarily evaluative and devaluing ecumenical ecclesiology can scarcely satisfy the other churches. Nevertheless it is adequate for the moment as a basis for co-operation, in evangelization among other fields. Applied to evangelization, it means that the Catholic Church recognizes the evangelizing work of the others as legitimate and, ultimately, is prepared to support it.

In this connection specific rules and guidelines have been worked out jointly. The process began in the 1950s with the member churches of the World Council, as more and more Orthodox churches joined. They pressed for a clarification of the problem of proselytization: that is, the passive or actively provoked movement of Christians from one church to another. The first result of the discussion was a report entitled 'Christian Witness, Proselytism and Religious Liberty', which was officially accepted by the General Assembly of the World Council of Churches in New Delhi in 1961.[3] The document condemns any form of deliberate enticement of members of other churches while at the same time upholding the right of individuals to move from one ecclesial community to another as a result of a decision of conscience. This marked out the main boundaries on either side within which a joint witness can develop.

As a result of the ecumenical opening brought about by the Second

Vatican Council, a Joint Theological Commission was set up in 1968 with the agreement of representatives of the Catholic Church and the World Council of Churches and with the task of studying the problems.[4] The commission continued to build on the old foundations, but this time on a broader ecumenical basis. It rejected any form of proselytism, confirmed freedom of conscience and called for joint witness: Unity in witness and witness in unity. This is the will of Christ for his people. . . . All Christian communions, in spite of their divisions, can have a positive role to play in God's plan of salvation. . . . The central task of the Churches is simply to proclaim the saving deeds of God. This then should be the burden of their common witness; and what unites them is enough to enable them in large measure to speak as one' (ibid.). The commission's main achievement was the preparation of detailed principles for mutually acceptable behaviour. These include a condemnation of 'any form of physical force, moral coercion or psychological pressure . . . any overt or covert offer of temporal or material advantage . . . any exploitation of poverty, weakness or lack of education . . . anything which casts suspicion on the 'good faith' of the other . . . any unjust or uncharitable references to beliefs or behaviour of other religious communities as a means to win adherents for one's own' (ibid.). These rules of conduct were also applied, not just to intra-ecumenical witness between Christian churches, but also to the joint work of preaching in the world. In other words, the churches had gone beyond questions of principle and reached agreement on the basis of a sort of ethic of collaboration in mission and evangelization.

Nevertheless, even in the last seven years there has been no progress worth mentioning in practical co-operation. Both in the traditional Christian countries and in predominantly non-Christian areas, occasional attempts to plan and carry out evangelization jointly remain, as far as I can see, the great exception. The main reason for this seems to me to be difficulties in the field of practical ecclesiology, especially the problem of church membership. People won over by evangelization must inevitably join one of the churches.[5] At this point, if not before, the common path divides. Together with the considerable differences in the style of work, this problem is a formidable barrier.

The Middle East Council of Churches, which is made up of the Eastern Orthodox, Orthodox and Protestant Churches, and with which the Catholic Churches co-operate, has a department of evangelization. The department has no difficulty in operating in areas concerned with the co-ordination of Christian publications and literature programmes or the organization of joint visiting in new housing developments in Cairo. Of particular importance is its work on an ecumenical Arabic translation of the Bible, to some extent as a preliminary to joint evangelization. But joint activity goes no further than this preliminary stage. When the question of church membership arises with people who show interest or new converts, the fact that Christians are in a minority can quite quickly turn it in practice into competition.

In an attempt to bring about progress in this practical work, the General Assembly in New Delhi some time ago asked the WCC Commission for World Mission and Evangelization to produce a programme with the title 'Joint Action for Mission'. The aim was to take limited geographical areas or social sectors, plan their evangelization jointly and to commit the forces of all the Christian communities and church institutions represented in them in a co-ordinated way. A series of planning conferences was subsequently held in the 1960s in the Far East and West Africa. However, a joint programme could only be implemented in exceptional cases, mainly in areas previously untouched by the churches such as the new industrial city of Durgapur in northern India, or Formosa.[6] The practical ecclesiological difficulties previously outlined acted here too as enormous obstacles. D.T. Niles, the well-known Asian ecumenist, summed up the problem as follows: 'It will be necessary to fashion organs and procedures of partnership whereby there is achieved not simply joint consultation but joint decision in all matters concerning the mission of the Church'.[7]

EVANGELIZATION AS A THEOLOGICAL PROBLEM

Niles, who until 1960 headed the Department on Evangelism in Geneva, also points out that in large parts of the Christian world there is no sense of the urgency of evangelization. He thus draws attention to theological problems which lie several levels deeper than the practical difficulties. They clearly concern the totality of theological interpretation and the existence of the Church in the modern world, involving such basic questions as the communication of the Gospel, uniqueness and the claim to absoluteness, the meaning of salvation, and so on. From the multitude of these theological topics I have selected two which seem to me to be particularly acute in current ecumenical discussion. The discussion, which is often heated, is not in these cases divided along denominational boundaries, but cuts across all the churches. My examples are taken from the part of the Christian world I know best.

At the WCC General Assembly in Uppsala in 1968 a typical dispute broke out about evangelization over the question of the 'two billion'. The argument was about the aim of evangelization. Should it press ahead and use all the churches' resources to evangelize the hundreds of millions of non-Christians not yet reached, or only inadequately reached, by the Christian message. Or is it more important to manifest the salvation offered in the Gospel by the example of living faith and renewed life, and to seek to establish a representative presence of the Church in every culture and among all human groups as a *pars pro toto*? This dispute has still not ended. It helped to bring about the polarization between 'evangelicals' and 'ecumenists' at the beginning of the seventies which threatened at its peak to develop into a new schism in Protestantism.

Since the World Conference on Evangelization at Lausanne in 1974, on the one hand, and the Assembly of the WCC in Nairobi in 1975, on the other, the language has become less extreme and there has been a greater tendency to work through the differences in discussion.[8] It has been recognized that evangelization cannot consist simply in verbal proclamation, but must always be accompanied by Christian social action. The renewal of the Church thus becomes part of the task of world evangelization. On the other hand it is stressed that the urgency of the renewal of the Church as a precondition for the credibility of its missionary commitment does not affect the urgency of the task of preaching the whole Gospel to all men. The conflict of aims is, however, still far from being resolved by such eirenical statements. Its resolution must include a theological working through of the Constantinian era of Church history with its quantitative ideas of the Christianization of the earth. It must include the solution which is right for us to the brief hymnic formula of Mt 28, with a view to a reversal of emphasis as between the two key terms 'make disciples' and 'all nations'. Is evangelization measured primarily by numerical criteria? Does it try to reach as many individuals as possible? Or is the main goal of evangelization to stimulate authentic discipleship as measured by qualitative criteria, which will then work in all nations like 'salt' and 'leaven'?

A second controversial subject in the ecumenical discussion can be seen in the dispute about the primary context of evangelization. Traditional evangelization in western Protestantism, for example, has been directed primarily at the individual, and called him or her to decision and repentance. Conversion was the real aim in 'evangelical' circles, and the experience of conversion, even including the precise location of the moment of conversion, took on particular importance. The context here is a particular individualistic view of man. In contrast to this, other theologians and representatives of new forms of evangelization see man as a social being existing primarily in the network of his social relationships. Here the immediate context is the social group or class, which is embedded in socio-economic structures and a particular social system.

In this dispute too the differences have decreased. No one, for example, denies that the message of the Gospel has a personal meaning. Nevertheless, according to where priorities lie, there are still very different models of evangelization, with very different theological bases. In one concern is primarily with the person, and evangelization is the communication of a message which imparts truth and conveys meaning, calls for a change of outlook and offers membership of a community. In the other view the most important aspect is the permeation of a situation with the Gospel. This means preaching as the offer of liberation and the presentation of an alternative pattern of behaviour. This means social action as the incarnation of the Word and therefore not just as an implication of preaching, but as its core. This means solidarity with whoever are the oppressed and with the poor. It means taking sides. In the words of the Bolivian Manifesto on evangelization in Latin America: 'Through its content, nature and aims, evangelization creates conflicts in the hearer, in the witness and in society. Evangelization does not identify with any party programme, nor does it present the Church as an alternative force. But, when it preaches the word of God and projects the light of that word on to human history, that has inevitable political consequences.'[9]

THE UNDISPUTED NEED FOR RENEWAL

Amid all the still unsolved ecumenical problems in evangelization, it is undisputed that a renewal in all the Churches is necessary if they are to take their task of evangelization seriously today. Philip Potter ended his address to the Episcopal Synod in Rome with a reference to a remark by a Catholic speaker: 'A church which is being renewed in order more effectively to evangelize is a church which is itself willing to be evangelized.' Potter added, 'In reality, evangelization, renewal and unity are intimately related as the common calling of all the churches. Evangelization is the test of our ecclesiastical vocation. The crisis we are going through today is not so much a crisis of faith as a crisis of faithfulness of the whole people of God.'[10]

Translated by F. McDonagh

Notes

1. Point 10 of the declaration, translated from the German text in *Herder Korrespondenz* 28 (1974), p. 623.

2. Secretariat for Promoting Christian Unity, *Information Service* 25, 1974/III, pp. 1-6.

3. Text in *Evanston—New Delhi, Report of the Central Committee to the Third Assembly* (Geneva, 1961), pp. 239ff.

4. Text: *Third Official Report of the Joint Working Group,* Appendix II.

5. In accordance with international usage, 'evangelization' here refers to the preaching of the Christian faith as the core of mission, and not to work among nominal Christians.

6. Cf. C.H. Hwang, *Joint Action for Mission,* World Council of Churches (Formosa, 1968).

7. D.T. Niles, *Upon the Earth* (London, 1962), p. 157.

8. Cf. the Lausanne Commitment and the report of Section I of the Nairobi General Assembly.

9. Translated from: *Monatlicher Informationsbrief über Evangelisation* (WCC, Geneva), No. 2/25, p. 7.

10. Mgr. Etchegaray; cf. n. 2, p. 6.

Michael Singleton and Henri Maurier

The Establishment's Efforts to Solve the Evangelical Energy Crisis: The Fourth Roman Synod and *Evangelii Nuntiandi*

HEADS OF STATE either beg to differ about the world's energy problems or have their discordant voices harmonized by last night commit-
tees. Even supposing one of their number possessed sufficient stamina,
time and expertise, his colleagues would find it unnatural that he com-
pose single-handed a final statement. Today, the most efficient and
democratically normal way of producing a satisfactory declaration, is
for a competent team to thrash out its terms in common. Though representing an organization which considers itself divinely obliged to respect all that is natural, heads of local Churches forming the Catholic
communion, surprisingly ignored this elementary principle of sound
procedure when they met in Rome, October 1974, to discuss their
evangelical energy crisis. Rather than seek a collegial way out of the
cul-de-sac in which they eventually found themselves, the bishops
deposited their deliberations at the feet of an ailing pontiff, leaving him
to sort out their differences as best he could. Under the circumstances,
it was to be expected that the Pope should take more than a year to
come up with *Evangelii Nuntiandi* and that his Apostolic Exhortation,
though echoing the Synod's debates, falls short of solving them.[1]

Since their futility frustrates not a few of those who make them,[2] the
problem is not so much whether magisterial pronouncements are effec-

113

tive as why they are not. Some blame the stoniness of the ground, others suspect that the sowers might be too removed from it. The stumbling-blocks towards that deliberative co-responsibility and democratic accountability which could make hierarchical harangues evangelically more convincing are not only structural. Ideological inadequacies are as formidable an obstacle as monarchical power structures. Consequently the ambiguities affecting the idiom employed by the ecclesiastical establishment to reactivate apostolic energies must be examined before institutional improvements can be made operative.

The ecstatic commentaries once reserved for papal pronouncements have given way to more discriminating studies. Encyclicals have been subject to structuralist analyses and the discrepancies between past and present positions of the magisterium examined.[3] The exhortatory genre of *Evangelii Nuntiandi* precludes any such sophisticated and punctilious criticism. The Pope's intention was to 'encourage' and 'confirm' his bishops in their missionary mandate and to share with their flocks his 'meditation on evangelization'.

A general, galvanizing his flagging army into fighting fitness, can hardly be faulted for making light of adverse odds. *Evangelii Nuntiandi,* designed to mobilize, understandably does not dwell in detail on those difficulties, which, though raised at the Synod, could demoralize the papal troops at large. What has happened to the Catholic Church in the Far East and what is happening to it in parts of America or Africa, suggest, however, that less sanguine missiological perspectives than the expansionist ones of the Apostolic Exhortation might eventually be needed.

It could be objected that in say China or Mozambique, the Church simply finds herself once more in the catacombs. Having weathered out the storm of persecution before, is there any reason why the barque of Peter should not put out to sea again and finally accomplish its divine mission of inviting all mankind aboard? Missionaries in Algeria, however, no longer envisage evangelization in this manner. 'Any expansionist missiology is concretely out of line in a country whose inhabitants are firmly determined to remain what they are: Muslims'.[4] Nor are they convinced when outsiders talk of a leaven which will raise the dough of Islam to unsuspected heights, or speak of a seed which will blossom into a fully-fledged Church. They wonder whether Christianity alone is capable of 'effectively establishing with God an authentic and living relationship' (53). They are not sure whether Christ had any particular ecclesial fruit in mind, let alone that peculiar kind, centred on the sacramental ministry of a parish clergy (58), when he spoke of God's kingdom. The desacramentalization of the priestly ministry and the relocation of the ecclesial centre of gravity in basic communities which the Church of Algeria had time to think its way towards, has been suddenly forced, by the circumstances of radical socialist revolutions, upon other churches.[5]

A politician, whipping up enthusiasm for his policies, cannot be blamed for dwelling on the opposition's weaknesses and turning a blind eye to the mistakes of his own party. Had the Pope wanted to make a scholarly contribution to missiological theory, he would probably have drawn the lessons which some Third World bishops feel the darker sides of mission history teach.[6] Paul VI presumably did not want to distract his reader's meditation with historical asides about the Inquisition or Crusades, when he apodictically asserts that the 'Church cannot accept violence, especially the force of arms . . . and indiscriminate death as the path to liberation' (37). Likewise, had *Evangelii Nuntiandi* been a balanced encyclical rather than an impassioned sermon, the plea that Catholics be allowed religious freedom (39) would perhaps have been prefaced by an apology for the Church's former intolerance. Seeing that the Pope concludes that 'it is an error to impose something on the conscience of our brethren' (80), his plea might even have been followed up by some concrete gesture such as the refusal to put pressure on individuals and institutions which do not toe the hierarchical line—after all, as *Evangelii Nuntiandi* insists, deeds are as eloquent as words.

When even the advocates of lost causes can be carried away by their own eloquence, one cannot take exception to *Evangelii Nuntiandi's* slight exaggeration of the demand for what it has to offer. It would be unfair to expect an exhortation to examine the market situation soberly. In terms of missions, however, the possibilities now seem less bright than previously. Most people the world over have by now made their choice, be it religious or a-religious, nor is it easy to detect everywhere that 'nostalgic emptiness' in which the Pope sees 'a powerful and tragic appeal' for evangelization (55). The de-Christianization of a society, which was in any case ambiguously Christianized, seems to some more a sign of secular strength than 'natural weakness' (56). Loving fathers are often pained by their sons' indifference to the things they hold sacred. The sons as brothers, however, might sincerely feel they have opted for more satisfactory values such as human rights or an optimistic Marxism.

This paternal solicitude to see sons re-united around traditional truths sets the tone of *Evangelii Nuntiandi*. 'Paul VI does not write as a theologian but as a supreme pastor. He does not seek precision of terminology but the reconciliation of opposing theologies'.[7] No one prefers disunity to unity. Models for union and the modalities of re-union vary, however, according to the position and propensities of individuals. As the incumbent of the Petrine office, the Pope tends to ride roughshod over those terminological niceties which theologians see as the indispensable steps towards reconciliation. The monarchical heads of hierarchical organizations are likely to have a model of unity in their minds which caters less creatively for conflict than the patterns upon which those at the periphery act. Paul VI's reticence towards the theological pluralism which resurfaced during the Synod, is well known. Where he fears a diversification of belief and behaviour which could lead to sectarianism (48) some missiologists have seen in sects themselves a unique chance for Christ. Indigenous Christian movements in the Third World have related the Gospel to the oppressed in a way mainline, monolithic churches have proved incapable of doing. The effects of disunity between the churches or within the same church, inevitably seem more disastrous from the monarchical top than the popular bottom of the hierarchical pyramid.

Time will tell whether the price for employing the exhortatory rather than the encyclical style was too high. For the time being, the establishment's press reports that the Apostolic Exhortation has given the front line troops the fillip they sorely needed. Gaining a victory is one thing, winning a war another. While one cannot but rejoice in the encouragement hard pressed apostles already in the field have received, one wonders whether the apostolic energies of the emerging generation will be sufficiently stimulated by the Pope's more theoretical assumptions.

The Pope's thinking about the missions naturally surfaces in the categoric contrasts of his own theological tradition: material/spiritual (27), temporal/eternal (28), immanent/transcendent (70), socio-economic/purely pastoral (31, 33), secular/religious (32), natural/supernaturally revealed religion (53), priests/people (66-70) with its panoply of supporting similes: father/children, shepherd/sheep, the passive objects of pastoral activists.[8]

Whereas most Catholic theologians would once have subscribed to these dichotomies, many are now experimenting with alternatives. Rather than suppose that belief in spirits is, mutatis mutandis, superior to disbelief, could not a more relevant line be drawn between subjectivistics, pseudo-spiritualities and a healthy humanism? Should the decisive distinction be made between those who do and those who do not accept the existence of heaven, hell and a personal God, or between those who are content and those who are discontented with closed systems, whatever their cultural contours? While 'not every notion of liberation is necessarily consistent and compatible with an evangelical vision of man' (35), does not the dissociation of socio-economic development and purely religious salvation echo too closely the de facto division between laity and clergy? Does not the equation of direct evangelization with the sacramental activities of the priest and the relegation of lay endeavours to the level of an indirect apostolate, answer more to the medieval creation of a clerical caste than to anything known in New Testament times? Would not the superiority of Christianity be more palatable as 'outstanding in its class' than as 'in a totally different class of its own'? If one began and ended with the People of God, would not more egalitarian and less mystifying notions of Christian ministry materialize than those manifest in n.58?

The issues which divided the Synod constitute the crux of *Evangelii Nuntiandi:* conversion to Christ, the relating of Revelation to other cultures and the ecclesial element in evangelization. With regard to each, the Pope spells out admirably what is axiomatically at stake. One cannot but agree with his firm restatement of fundamental principles. Where some will find it difficult to follow his reasoning, is when these non-negotiable absolutes are equated, apodictically, with ideas and institutions they deem relative and dispensable.[9]

The exordium of *Evangelii Nuntiandi* could hardly be more evangelical. Christ figures substantially from the outset and in a way which Christian radicals, to left or right, could not but applaud. The Church must constantly re-align herself on Christ, otherwise her claim to convert others would be compromised (15). Conversion is explicitly to Christ—the Pope makes little mention of such psycho-sociologically incredible theologoumena as were 'anonymous Christians' or 'implicit members of the Mystical Body'. The unbeliever must be put into contact with Christ by the words and deeds of committed Christians: 'Is there any way of handing on the Gospel than by transmitting to another person one's personal experience of faith?' (46). Though there can be but one answer to this question, what happens when the personal experience in question is that of a Hans Küng or Fernando Belo[10] and when the other person is a Pygmy or Papuan? Between the axiomatic absoluteness of Christ, on the one hand, and on the other, the determination of what exactly is to be handed over and what the ecclesial embodiment of this Christian experience should be, is a gap about whose dimensions some hesitate.

There is a prima facie radicalness in *Evangelii Nuntiandi's* understanding of the relationship between revelation and the cultural context. The Gospel is described in dynamic terms, as a living substance, full of power and energy (4:25). It must be enabled to reach the roots of other cultures and not be simply stuck on the surface (20). The depth to which the Church is prepared to allow Christ to reincarnate himself elsewhere seems compromised, however, by recourse to epistemological categories in which a theology of revelation was once couched. In the pope's opinion, there exists 'an unchangeable deposit of faith' (65) whose 'essential contents' (25, 63) are fully preserved in their 'untouchable purity' (3) by the Roman Catholic magisterium alone (54). When the core of revelation is so hard and so assuredly held, there seems to be little hope of any substantial feedback from the context, upon the idiom and institutions of Roman Catholic Christianity. Not a few of the synod fathers, by contrast, felt that the Church had much to learn from the world at large.

Few could fail to be moved by the pope's meditation on the universal Church (61) and its essentially missionary dimension (14, 15, 23, 24). Misgivings could arise in some minds, however, at the continuities established by *Evangelii Nuntiandi* between the kingdom of God, the Roman Catholic Church, the parish church and the sacerdotal-sacramental ministry (58, 64).

In pinpointing the equivocal presuppositions of magisterial attempts to re-animate missionary fervour, it has not been intended to indicate any univocal solution to the issues involved. On the contrary, the socio-cultural diversities within and between the Catholic Churches preclude the emergence of substantially similar solutions. It is perhaps only when this irreducible divergence has dawned upon the ecclesiastical authorities that measures will be taken to create an overarching organization, able to cater constructively for a potentially enriching diversity. New sources of evangelical energy have materialized recently—charismatic movements, Christians for Socialism, Third World theologies, and so on. Without a framework more flexible than the one at present in force, the Second Pentecost, which is invariably in question when ecclesiastics gather, will never take place. The First Pentecost was not organized by the elderly males who formed the largely clerical and exclusively Jewish Establishment of the year 33. The Spirit burst forth amongst young lay people of both sexes and from every tribe and tongue. The Roman Catholic Church's efforts to make Christ count for others will continue to be equivocally effective until such a time as youth, women, the laity and non-westerners come to shape its destiny more decisively.

Notes

1. For the issues raised during the Synod, cf. R. Laurentin, *L'Evangelisation après le quatrième Synode* (Paris, 1975) and the special notes 33 and 36 of *Pro Mundi Vita* (Brussels, 1974). Among the synodal topics not explicitly treated by Paul VI are the emancipation of women and human rights.

2. Archbishop Hurley: 'Sermons and pastoral letters are the lowest form of human communication', *The Tablet* (3.1.1976).

3. E.g., F. Houtart, 'Stratégie pontificale et société internationale', pp. 115-33 and J. Matthes, 'La doctrine sociale de l'Eglise comme système de connaissance', pp. 135-54, in *La pratique de la théologie politique*, ed. M. Xhaufflaire (Tournai, 1974); P.M. Dioudonnaté, 'Pouvoir et Providence: sur quelques variations de la politique des évêques de France', in *Contrepoint* 15 (September 1974), pp. 175-87.

4. H. Sanson, 'Chrétiens en Algérie', in *Christus* XXII 86 (April 1975), p. 214.

5. The Pope is persuaded that the parish constitutes the key, lower level, ecclesial structure (58) and that basic communities are more prone to political deviation than larger Churches.

6. Cardinal Malula, in his intervention of 2.10.1974, on behalf of the Zairean episcopacy, spoke of the Catholic Church having been one of the pillars of the colonial system. Rome condoned slavery right up to the middle of the last century; cf., J.F. Maxwell, *Slavery and the Catholic Church* (London, 1975).

7. J. Snijders, 'Evangelii Nuntiandi: the movement of minds', in *The Clergy Review* LXII 5 (1977), p. 171.

8. Though popular religion often carries protest against the political and priestly status quo, *Evangelii Nuntiandi* simply states that the people's piety must be directed from on high (48).

9. Cf., H. Maurier, 'La théologie chrétienne des religions non-chrétiennes' in *Lumen Vitae* XXXI 1 (1976), p. 93 for this ambiguous absoluteness, which is no longer that of Christ but that of individual and institutional pride.

10. H. Küng, *Being a Christian* (New York & London, 1977), esp. section C. 1; F. Belo, *Lecture matérialiste de l'évangile de Marc* (Paris, 1974).

Contributors

DURAISAMY AMALORPAVADASS was born in India in 1932. He is founder-Director of the National Biblical, Catechetical and Liturgical Centre of India, and Secretary of three National Episcopal Commissions for liturgy, catechetics and the Bible. He has been a member of the RCC-WCC Joint Working Group since 1976. He is founder-editor of two monthly reviews and has published or edited many books and articles.

JOSEF AMSTUTZ was born in 1927. Since 1967 he has been Director of the Bethlehem Missionary Society at Immensee in Switzerland. He has taught at the Schöneck Missionary Seminary and at Fribourg University as well as at the theological faculty of the University of Lucerne.

FERNANDO CASTILLO was born in 1943 and studied theology and sociology in Santiago, Chile, Münster and Sussex, England. He taught at the Catholic University of Chile and has published on the ideology and theology of liberation.

HEINZGÜNTER FROHNES studied history, sociology and theology in Freiburg im Breisgau, Heidelberg and Tübingen. He is editor of the nine-volume *Kirchengeschichte als Missionsgeschichte*.

ALEXANDRE GANOCZY was born in 1928. He studied in Budapest, Paris and at the Gregorian. He is Professor of Systematic Theology at Würzburg University and he has published books and articles on Calvin, the Church, God-language and creativity.

WALTER J. HOLLENWEGER was born in 1927. He studied at Zürich and Basle, and since 1971 he has been Professor of Missiology at the University of Birmingham. He has published many books and articles on Pentecostalism, evangelization and the charismatic movement.

PAUL LÖFFLER was born in 1931. He is an Evangelical theologian. He was Professor of Missiology and Ecumenics at the Near East School of Theology in Beirut and is now Director of Studies at the Missionary Academy of the University of Hamburg. He has published on conversion, mission, and proselytism.

HENRI MAURIER is a White Father and was born in 1921. He has been a professor of philosophy at various seminaries, and a missionary for ten years in the Upper Volta. He has published widely on the theology of paganism, religion and African tradition, and the philosophy of Black Africa, and since 1970 he has been leader of the seminar on African pastoral work at the Lumen Vitae Institute in Brussels.

NORBERT METTE was born in 1946. He studied theology and social sciences and is research assistant at the Pastoral Theology Seminar of the University of Münster. He has published on the history and theory of practical theology and on practical pastoral questions.

TAMÁS NYÍRI was born in 1921. He studied in Perugia, Budapest and Vienna. He is a professor at the Roman Catholic Theological Academy in Budapest. He is a member of the editorial committee of the monthly *Vigilia*. He has published on the Christian mission in the world, anthropology and philosophic thought, and he is Hungarian delegate to the Secretariat for Non-Believers.

PHEME PERKINS is Associate Professor of New Testament at Boston College. She has published on the Gospel of John and an Introduction to the New Testament as well as on Gnosticism and NT theology. She is a member of the editorial boards of the *Catholic Biblical Quarterly* and the *Journal of Biblical Literature*.

YVES RAGUIN, S.J., was born in 1912. He went to Shanghai in 1949, and worked on Chinese foreign-language dictionaries. He was Professor of Chinese History at Saigon National University, and of Buddhist Philosophy at Dalat Catholic University. He is Professor of Non-Christian Religions in the Catholic University of Fujen, the East Asian Pastoral Institute, Manila, and at the Institute of East Asia Spirituality, Fujen. He has published on mission, Buddhism and Christianity, and the Spirit.

MICHAEL SINGLETON was born in 1939 and studied with the White Fathers, then at the Gregorian, and primitive religion at Oxford. He spent 1969-72 studying spirit possession in an *ujamaa* village in Tanzania. He has published on African religion and anthropology.

PIERRE TALEC was born in 1933. Since 1973 he has been in charge of the Jean-Bart Centre in Paris. He has published on pastoral work, belief, catechetics, and mission. He has broadcast in France and Canada and has published poems and records.

MARCELLO ZAGO was born in 1932. He was a missionary in Laos and has published on Buddhist rites and ceremonies and evangelization. He was guest professor in missiology at San Paolo University, Ottawa, and is Professor of Missiology at the Lateran in Rome.